Smart House

THE COMING REVOLUTION IN HOUSING

R A L P H   L E E   S M I T H

Smart House

THE COMING REVOLUTION IN HOUSING

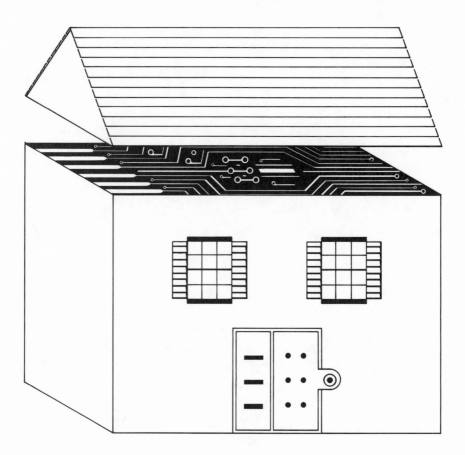

GP PUBLISHING
Columbia, Maryland

GP Publishing, Inc.
10650 Hickory Ridge Road
Columbia, MD 21044
(301) 964-6253

Library of Congress Cataloging-in-Publication Data

Smith, Ralph Lee, 1927-
    Smart house.

    1. Dwellings—Automation.   2. Dwellings—
Electronic equipment.   I. Title.
TH4812.S63   1987   643'.6   87-21262
ISBN 0-87683-918-9
ISBN 0-87683-919-7 (pbk.)

The term SMART HOUSE, together with the associated star symbol that appears in Figure 1, is a registered service mark of the Smart House Development Venture, Inc. In this book, the term Smart House, with initial letters in caps, is used to describe the intelligent home energy and communications system being developed by the Smart House Development Venture under this service mark.

The following organizations and individuals have generously given permission to reprint their copyrighted materials: *EPRI Journal*, for the quotation on pp. 11-12, from "The Smart House: Wired for the Electronic Age," by Taylor Moore (November 1986). *Potomac Electric Power Company*, for figure 18. *National Association of Home Builders National Research Center*, for the illustrations and photographs in figures 4, 7-11, 17, and 23. *NAHB National Research Center and Spyder Webb*, for the illustrations in figures 2, 3, 5-16, and 19-22. *NAHB National Research Center and Marchant and Faulkner*, for the artist's drawing in figure 1.

Contents

1
The Coming of
the Smart House

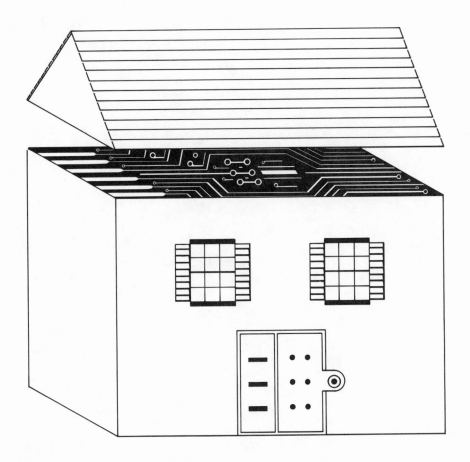

In April 1987, ground was broken for the world's first Smart House. With the building of this house (Figure 1), one of the last major frontiers of the information age was breached. In the 1990s, semiconductors, the tiny components used in computers, communications equipment, television sets, VCRs, and advanced electronics, will enter the wiring of homes. Entirely new wiring systems and new hardware will accommodate the chips.

Within ten years after this ground breaking, it is estimated that more than 8 million American and Canadian homes and light-frame buildings will contain intelligent wiring systems. Home devices and appliances will contain semiconductors— "chips"—that will enable them to communicate with the wiring network, with each other, and with the outside world. Homes will have caught up with nearly everything else in our society that employs electrical and gas energy—they will become "smart."

As with other major technological developments of the electronic age, the coming of the Smart House will have many impacts on American life, not all of which can be known or

Figure 1. Artist's drawing of the first Smart House

foreseen. Some forecasters stress the Smart House's ability to offer levels of convenience and comfort that are unavailable in homes today, although such conveniences are part of broader capabilities and a broader story.

Smart House Scenarios

Taylor Moore, writing in the *EPRI Journal*, provides the following look into the near-future, which he describes as "one of many possible scenarios that may be commonplace to new homeowners in the 1990s":

> Half an hour before you rise, the water heater turns on to reach just the right temperature in time for your shower. Bedroom and bathroom lights turn on as the radio wakeup alarm sounds. The rooms you use at that hour have been preheated. The coffee maker comes on while you're in the shower; when you finish, you're greeted by a full pot, and the television is on with your favorite news show.
>
> During the day, as it warms up outside, the air conditioner keeps the indoor air comfortable if anyone is home but avoids running during a two-hour afternoon peak period when electricity rates are the highest; the dishwasher that was loaded the night before runs itself early in the morning. A security system keeps watch while you're away but decides not to call the police when a neighborhood kid tosses the evening paper against the front door.
>
> When you return, recorded telephone messages are played back over the bedroom speakers while you change, but soothing music fills the den where you relax. A flashing light on a video screen announces that dinner in the microwave is ready. As dusk falls,

outdoor lights turn on, the garden sprinkler gives the begonias a drink, and during commercials on the evening news you watch a display on the screen of the day's energy consumption and costs.

Before you retire, the screen provides a status check of all outside doors and locks. The house turns off all nonessential appliances that were on, save for the reading lamp over the bed. Room occupancy sensors automatically light the hall and kitchen if you venture out of bed for a nocturnal glass of milk.

Figure 2 is a drawing provided by the Smart House Development Venture, Inc. The Venture, which is described in the next chapter, is serving as the coordinating group for the creation of Smart House hardware and appliances. Various capabilities of the Smart House are keyed to numbers in the drawing.

1. When an appliance is plugged in, it identifies itself to the network as an item that is eligible to receive current. This communication between the appliance or device and the network is achieved by means of a chip in the appliance that is capable of communicating with a chip in the network. Unless and until an appliance containing a chip that can communicate this information with the network is plugged in, there is no current available at the outlet. A baby sticking its finger, or a metallic object, into a Smart House outlet will not be harmed because neither the child nor the metallic object contains a communicating chip.

2. The Smart House instantly cuts off current to the hair dryer that has been accidentally dropped into the bathroom basin. The capability of cutting off power instantly wherever there is an overload, a short-circuit, or an accidental grounding, as is the case with the hair dryer, exists for every outlet in the home.

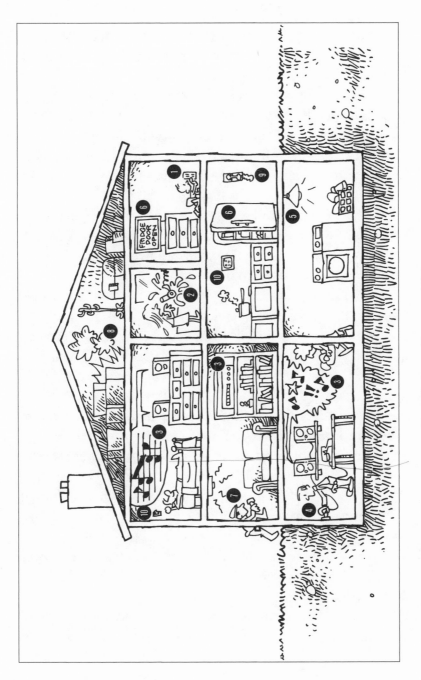

Figure 2. Smart House capabilities

3. Stereo speakers can be plugged directly into any outlet in the house without running additional wiring. In the drawing, the stereo receiver in the living room is providing music to speakers located in both the bedroom and the basement. In case of fire, anything being played on the speakers could be overridden by a spoken alarm.

4. Any Smart House device can be plugged into any outlet in the house. A person in the basement can unplug the stereo speaker and plug a telephone into the same outlet to make a call.

5. The Smart House can be instructed to turn off lights when a person leaves the room, and turn them on when the person reenters. Similar instructions can be given to regulate the temperature in unused rooms.

6. Smart House systems can employ one or more video display screens in convenient locations, which will monitor the status of appliances and devices. These screens can provide an alert when, for example, the refrigerator door has been left open, ovens or stove burners have been left on, or the front door is unlocked.

7. Sensors placed throughout the house can activate an alarm when an intruder enters. However, a dog walking through the house at night, or an inveterate midnight snacker heading for the refrigerator, would not trip the alarm. The location of sensors need not be permanently fixed. When planning a trip or vacation, homedwellers could even rent a package of sensors and plug them into any outlets.

8. Sensors anywhere in the house can also detect smoke or fire. The same or other sensors can be used to regulate heating and cooling.

9. All systems in the house can be activated or controlled remotely by telephoning instructions from any location. At an appropriate time before leaving work, a Smart House

owner could instruct the air-conditioning system to bring the house temperature to a comfortable level and could tell the oven to turn on and start cooking dinner.

10. All appliances and devices attached to the system can be given instructions from a switch or other control device anywhere in the house. A switch, or even a telephone, placed next to a bed can be used to lock all doors and windows at night, and to instruct a stereo system to wake you up and a coffee maker to start operating in the morning. Downstairs heat can be raised a half-hour before you awaken.

The arrival of Smart House is the result of two major forces—one a "push" and one a "pull." The push is provided by increasingly serious shortcomings in the wiring of today's homes. The pull is provided by the inevitable course of developments in modern electronics. Increasingly, electrical devices are becoming smart, and increasingly, they are being linked together in communication networks.

In this book, to secure a clear view of Smart House, we will begin by looking at these two converging forces, and we will review the obstacles that retarded the coming of Smart House despite both the logic and the power of these forces.

We will then explain in basic terms how the Smart House works. In the process, we will answer a few questions about new communications technologies and how they work.

Finally, we will review and comment on some likely uses and benefits that can be foreseen. This review will take account of the contribution the Smart House can make to more comfortable living. It will also consider some capabilities of the technology that have broader social value and should be given prominence in planning and development.

2
The Wire Mire

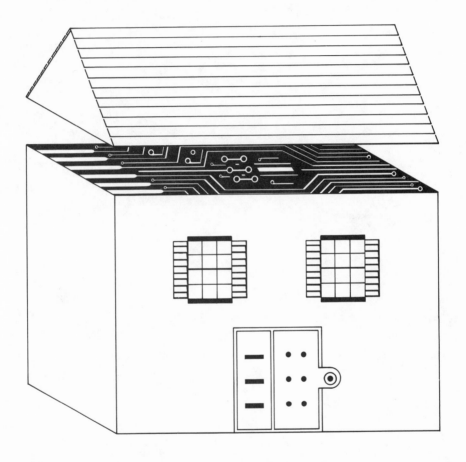

Virtually the only basic thing that has been done to the wiring of homes since Thomas Edison's day has been to proliferate the number of wiring systems that snake around the walls, and to increase the number and variety of devices that are attached to them. The result has been an ever-increasing tangle of spaghetti on both sides of the walls. Increasingly, the consequences involve more than the offending of orderly minds.

Within the past twenty years the tangle has been steadily growing. Homes which had one telephone just twenty years ago are now likely to have three or four. Some homeowners have installed security systems, requiring a whole new wiring network. Twenty years ago only a small percentage of homes had cable TV; now half of all homes have it. All of this is in addition not only to the basic house wiring, but to supplemental wiring for such items as doorbells and thermostats.

The prognosis is for continuing and unrelenting pressure on the wire mire. Consumer electronic products continue to be introduced. Meanwhile, to create a better balance of demand on their facilities, electric utilities are already experimenting with time-of-day pricing, which can be facilitated by new and better electronics in the home. The natural gas industry is conducting research on new portable appliances that could be plugged in at various places around the home, to outlets that combine a flexible gas pipe with electronic controls.

In addition to being increasingly obsolescent, the wire mire is growing more costly to create and maintain. A building contractor must usually call in several different wiring contractors to install the various systems, at a cost in duplicated activity that goes into the price of the house. The results achieved by this additional effort and expense are nothing great. No matter what is done, outlets never seem to end up where they are needed. Rooms are rearranged, telephones are moved to other tables, stereos end up in corners where there are no outlets. Festoons of octopus extension cords blossom along the baseboards. Circuit breakers pop when two appliances on the same circuit are turned on.

That things are still done this way is not a commentary on the limits of modern science. It is a commentary on the limits of where modern science has been able to reach. With the coming of Smart House, some well-established modern technology will enter an arena where it can really be of help. The tangles of wire will be replaced by a single cable incorporating several types of wires, including a coaxial cable for TV, standard wires for electrical energy, smaller wires for telephones and other low-voltage devices, and additional wires to accommodate digital signaling. This cable will be installed in new homes when they are built.

Universal outlets that will accommodate any appliance will be installed throughout the house. When the appliance is turned on or put into use, semiconductors in the house wiring system will communicate with semiconductors in the appliance and connect it to the appropriate circuit.

Problems of Electrical Safety

Another issue associated with today's wiring is electrical safety.

A great deal of thought, care, and effort has gone into reducing the hazards of having electrical wiring and electrical products in homes. These efforts have long been formalized in the activities of groups such as Underwriter's Laboratories and the National Electrical Code Committee of the National Fire Protection Association. The latter group maintains and updates the National Electric Code, comprising electrical safety guidelines that are widely accepted and followed.

Two important innovations of recent times have been the adoption of the third-wire ground and the introduction of devices called ground-fault circuit interrupters (GFIs).

Many people can remember when appliances such as washing machines were connected to a nearby water pipe with a wire and a clamp. After World War II this gave way to three-pronged plugs and outlets, with the third prong being a ground contact. In 1956 the National Electrical Code required such plugs and receptacles for laundry areas, breezeways, and garages, and in 1959 the coverage was extended to include exterior outlets, areas around kitchen sinks, basements, workshops, and open porches. However, a three-pronged outlet will accept a two-pronged plug with no ground. It was not until 1984 that the Code required most appliances and hand-operated tools to be grounded.

Ground-fault circuit interrupters are the second important safety innovation. GFIs are devices that shut off power to a circuit when current is being diverted from the circuit directly to the ground by some conductor such as a human body. The amount of current required to trip a GFI is much less than that required to trip a circuit breaker or blow a fuse.

When the skin is wet, the body's resistance to the conducting of electric current can drop to as little as one percent of the normal resistance of the body when dry. In 1971 the National Electrical Code was amended to require GFIs around swimming pools and in outdoor receptacles. Meanwhile, electrical appliances often used in bathrooms, such as hair dryers, shavers, curling irons, and "Water-piks," continued to proliferate in homes. In 1975 the Code was amended again to require GFIs in all receptacles in bathrooms. In 1987 the Code was amended again to require a GFI for at least one receptacle in the basement, and GFIs for receptacles in the kitchen that are within six feet of the sink and above the level of the counter top.

There are three problems associated with GFIs. One is that they should be manually tripped monthly to ensure that they are working properly. Many people do not bother. The second is that GFIs will sometimes trip themselves for no identifiable reason, to the great annoyance of homeowners. The third is the problem that is technically referred to as an unsafe failure mode. This means that if for any reason the GFI does *not* function when an emergency occurs, the victim is not protected from the continuing delivery of the current.

Despite these problems, a 1976 Department of Commerce report argued for the adoption of GFIs, stating that "requirements of ground fault protection on potentially dangerous outlets can save hundreds of lives annually." The GFI situation and the Department of Commerce's comment reflect both the importance of the electrical safety problem and the frustration of those who are doing their best to deal with it. A 1979 Consumer Products Safety Commission report estimates that 1,500 accidental electrocutions occur each year in the United States. CPSC also estimated that in 1983 there were more than 4,000 emergency room treatments for injuries, primarily burns, due to electric shock involving consumer products; an unknown additional number were treated by private physicians. Another CPSC document estimates that, in 1982, 192,000 residential fires, comprising 28 percent of the total, were caused by "electrical ignition." These fires resulted directly in 1,000 deaths and 13,000 injuries. Property loss was estimated at $923 million.

The toll is caused by two technical deficiencies of today's system. The first is that every branch and nerve of the wiring network is always activated. Electrical power is always present, up to every outlet and through the outlet into every cord of every lamp and appliance right up to the switch, even if the lamps and appliances are turned off. A child who sticks a bare metal object into an outlet will always receive a shock. The second problem is that the system usually has no way of knowing when something attached to it may not be performing properly. A malfunctioning appliance, power cord, or plug can be the cause of fire or death before a fuse will blow or a circuit breaker will trip.

Both of these problems are easily addressed if modern electronic technology is built into the wiring system. What is required is as follows:

- No current should be present at any outlet until an appliance is plugged in and turned on to receive the current. When nothing is plugged in and turned on, the outlet is dead.

- Anything that is plugged in and turned on should be able to *communicate* with the power distribution system.

- As long as the appliance is plugged in and turned on, its chip and the system chips should *remain in continuous communication*. Variance in the behavior of the appliance can then be communicated to the system, which can cut off current to that outlet.

Requirements of this type are met in many modern electronic systems. With the coming of Smart House, they will finally be met in the home.

Home Automation and Networking

Meanwhile, as we have noted, a second pressure was being brought to bear on home wiring systems—the simple but forceful pressure of electronic progress. The coming of Smart House is directly related to the increasing capability and decreasing price of semiconductors and microprocessors—that is, chips. Semiconductors provide communications and/or control capabilities. Microprocessors, which are a type of semiconductor, provide computing capability. Together they are virtually transforming the world, and in the long run there is no way that today's creaky home electrical system could escape.

Beginning in the early 1980s, semiconductors and microprocessors began to provide control and limited intelligence in a growing number of products, devices, and systems, including home entertainment products, microwave ovens, hot water systems, and heating, ventilation, and air-conditioning systems.

At the same time, semiconductors and microprocessors were increasingly employed in networks designed to link various kinds of products, devices, and systems together. In the commercial world, the trend included the introduction of so-called "intelligent buildings." In these buildings, intelligent wiring systems are installed at the time of construction, giving all networks access to communications systems and capabilities that would otherwise be beyond their reach.

It was of course understood that private homes, as well as commercial buildings, could be made smart. However, the problems were complex. In the commercial world, there were compelling bottom-line reasons for linking office machines together, and methods and protocols had been worked out to make communications among various devices possible. But chips in home appliances typically did not communicate with each other.

By the late 1970s some firms began to interest themselves in this frontier, and a small home-automation industry began to take shape. By 1985 home control devices and systems topped $300 million in retail sales. The systems and their capabilities are very diverse, but they generally employ central controllers, along with computer screens or push-button panels, to perform such functions as turning lights on and off and controlling the operation of appliances.

Formidable difficulties nevertheless remained. Systems with certain types of capabilities could use the existing wiring in the home as a communications link. Or, as an alternative, additional capabilities could be secured by partially rewiring homes with a network that was in addition to the existing home wiring. But neither approach offered the full range of capabilities that could be achieved by pursuing an approach that included, as parts of a unified plan, a new home wiring network and appliances designed to connect to it.

Unfortunately this, the most comprehensive solution, and in the long run the only really logical one, also entailed the greatest set of obstacles to its realization. This is the tale we will tell in the next chapter.

3
Breaking Down the Barriers

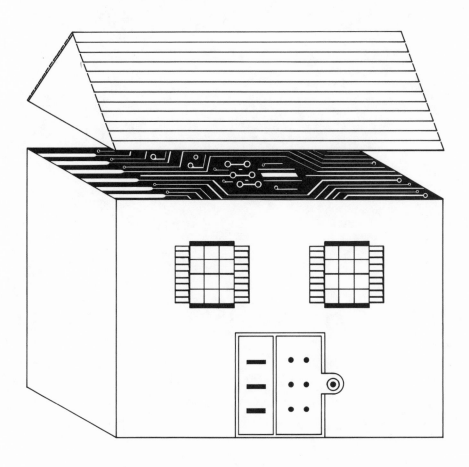

Ordinarily, an entrepreneur who is convinced that there is a niche or demand for a new product or technology, who has the assets, and who is willing to take the risks, can simply proceed to manufacture the product and put it on the market.

With Smart House, both the usefulness of the technology and its acceptability to consumers seem hardly subject to question. Yet the path from initial conception to marketing was beset with obstacles that many or most firms regarded as insurmountable.

If Smart House has such potential, why didn't a major firm go ahead to manufacture and market it a number of years ago?

The answer is that Smart House is not a single product. It comprises a very large number of products, developed and designed in accordance with a common plan that will enable them to function together with maximum capability and effectiveness. No one manufacturer—and, in fact, no two or three, however large—was in a position to design the system, produce all the network hardware, the communications hardware and the software, and a full range of appliances that could communicate with the network.

Granted that this is the case, why couldn't a number of manufacturers work together to create the Smart House? First, there was the question of who would run the show, acting as the conductor of this large and highly diversified orchestra. No volunteers for the role of conductor presented themselves.

Why not? This gets us into deep waters of American policy and tradition.

America is unique among major industrial nations in the hostility of its policies to commercial and industrial combinations. By contrast with many other countries, orchestration of multi-firm business undertakings has virtually no modern tradition in our highly individualistic commercial world. It does not reflect our approach to entrepreneurship, and there is a virtual total lack of relevant precedent, knowledge, or methodology.

There is of course a strong legal backbone beneath this aspect of American business, and that backbone is our antitrust laws. As a simple matter of fact, parties with relevant experience in horizontally or vertically organized business combinations might pay for the acquisition of knowledge and skill in this area by spending some time in jail.

The answers to the questions are therefore clear. No one firm could create Smart House. Two or more that tried to do it would probably have to spend more money on lawyers than on research, and even this might provide little protection. Companies with great interest and great faith in the Smart House concept might nevertheless think it safer not to even pick up the phone and discuss mutual efforts with other firms.

Finally, let us suppose that it was somehow possible to solve all these problems, and to design and manufacture a coordinated system consisting of the Smart House network and communicating devices and appliances. With the tremendous effort and investment made, what assurance would there then be that builders would abandon their present arrangements and install the system in new homes?

To compound the difficulty, few industries are as decentralized as homebuilding. Builders are generally in a position to think and act for themselves, and they are well known to do just that. A long time would have to pass before sufficient consumer pressure might develop to force the hand of members of an almost totally disaggregated industry, if they were not particularly interested.

The Role of David MacFadyen

By good fortune, one of the few people in the United States who occupied a strategically situated vantage point from which all the problems might be taken on, was fascinated by the idea of an intelligent house. That person was David J. MacFadyen, President of the NAHB (National Association of Home Builders) National Research Center. MacFadyen created the Smart House Project, domiciled it at the Research Center, and saw it successfully through the many complex and novel problems that stood in its way.

In the 1970s, MacFadyen was President of Technology & Economics (T&E), a Cambridge, Massachusetts, consulting firm. T&E's major clients included NASA and the Department of Housing and Urban Development. Through his work with these clients, MacFadyen became interested in a new technology called flat cable, which could be laid directly under carpets in commercial buildings, facilitating both original wiring and changes in wiring arrangements that might be made after tenants moved in.

The National Electrical Code did not recognize flat cable as a safe type of wiring, and this effectively prevented its use. MacFadyen was convinced that flat cable was safe. After a number of years, his energy and persistence paid off. He fully satisfied the Code writers that flat cable was safe, and provisions for its use were entered into the Code. Today it is widely used in commercial construction.

In the early 1980s, MacFadyen went to work for the NAHB National Research Center, and in 1984 he became the Center's President. By now another wiring matter was on his mind—Smart House. MacFadyen discussed the technical issues with Robert G. Edwards, a senior consultant at Oak Ridge National Laboratory. Responding to MacFadyen's questions, Edwards said that home wiring could be simplified, and could be made more safe. Since then Edwards has been a key figure in the development of Smart House technology.

The National Association of Home Builders is one of the largest trade associations in the world. Its 143,000 member-firms include 45,000 home building companies, who together account for some 90% of residential and 85% of commercial light frame construction in the United States. Other members include architects, contractors, manufacturers, and suppliers to the building trade. The Research Center is a wholly owned subsidiary of NAHB.

In the year that MacFadyen became President of the Research Center, another piece of the puzzle was falling into place. In 1984, both Congress and the Office for Productivity, Technology, and Innovation of the U.S. Department of Commerce were pondering the question of whether America's strict antitrust laws sometimes operated to place us at a disadvantage in international trade. Experts were particularly concerned with the impact of the antitrust laws in putting a damper on joint research and development, to create products that no one company could create by itself or to raise the level of technical knowledge among members of an industry.

Smart House was exactly the kind of important and constructive project that the experts had in mind, and to which existing laws posed virtually insuperable barriers.

MacFadyen spent a good deal of time with Dr. E. Bruce Merrifield, Assistant Secretary of Commerce and head of the Office for Productivity, Technology, and Innovation, and with other Department of Commerce officials as they participated in the framing of legislation to deal with the problem. In October Congress passed the National Cooperative Research Act of 1984, and President Reagan signed it into law. The law provided for an easing of antitrust restrictions that stood in the way of joint efforts among manufacturing firms to develop products that could stimulate the U.S. economy and be competitive in world markets. Under the law, a consortium can seek registration with the Department of Justice to carry out research and development efforts that are intrinsically difficult for any one firm to bring to fruition. If the consortium and its project are approved, they can go forward under guidelines in the Act that reduce their antitrust liability.

As soon as the law was passed, MacFadyen went into action. In November 1984, the NAHB National Research Center held a conference in Washington, D.C., on the Smart House idea. The response reflected great pent-up interest. Attendees included representatives of more than a hundred manufacturing firms, electric and gas utilities, trade associations, and government agencies with a relationship to the energy, communication, and home building industries. A number of major firms offered immediate support. The Smart House Project was established and became the first consortium for research and development that was formed under the new Act.

The project sought the participation of several manufacturers for every major type of hardware that would be needed for a Smart House system, and for every major appliance that would have to be redesigned to include communicating chips. Manufacturers were pleased to accept the NAHB National Research Center as orchestrator of the effort. By 1987 more than forty leading manufacturers had joined the project, and constituted its Steering Committee. A number of these signed research and licensing agreements to develop specific products under the general guidelines established by the consortium.

Some twenty-five other firms such as electric, gas, and telephone companies, trade associations, and firms that do not manufacture Smart House–related products but have a strong interest in the functioning of Smart House, joined the Smart House Advisory Committee. Two major industrial research organizations, the Electric Power Research Institute and the Gas Research Institute, joined the project as sponsors. A list of all firms and organizations involved in Smart House appears in Chapter 9.

At the same time, MacFadyen was marshaling the support of the building industry through the National Association of Home Builders. With sponsorship of the Smart House consortium coming from the building industry's own research arm, endorsement was quick and enthusiastic. NAHB voted to provide funding to the project to see it through its initial phases. Nearly 300 builders, including many of the nation's largest, signed commitments to install Smart House networks into the homes they build, as soon as the system is available.

As is evident from the stories of the adoption of requirements for third-wire grounds and GFIs and the granting of approval for flat cable, a number of years often or usually pass before the National Fire Protection Association includes a full set of provisions for a new technology in the National Electrical Code.

With Smart House, however, it was different. In 1986, NFPA took the almost unprecedented step of approving changes in the National Electrical Code to accommodate Smart House technology, even before the specific hardware existed. The action reflects both the established nature of the technology as it is now used in other applications, and the clear belief of the Code writers that intelligent home networks, rather than being another Band-Aid, represent a fundamental solution to serious problems. The new provisions appear in the 1987 edition of the Code.

Meanwhile, one of the project's two sponsors, the Gas Research Institute, undertook to provide financial support for the construction of a Laboratory Smart House. The Lab House is being used for hands-on research on the design of the network. In addition, research will be done on matters of particular interest to GRI. The house is located at NAHB's Research Home Park in Bowie, Maryland. As indicated at the beginning of the first chapter, it will become the first Smart House in the world.

As the project moved out of its initial stages, the NAHB National Research Center spun it off as a separately incorporated, profit-oriented entity called the Smart House Development Venture. David MacFadyen remained as Chairman of the Board and Chief Executive Officer. At the same time, in his continuing position as President of the Research Center, he was already focusing his dynamism on a broad new issue—the raising of quality standards throughout the U.S. home building industry to meet the increasing likelihood of international competition to the U.S. home builder on his own American turf.

The Smart House Development Venture is moving quickly to bring Smart House to market. About a year after completion of the Laboratory House, construction will begin on a number of prototype houses at locales throughout the United States. In these houses, advanced system integration will be tested, and operating features of the Smart House will be developed. At the same time, electric companies, gas companies, and telephone companies located in the geographical areas where the houses are built will do research to identify consumer interests and needs, and will begin to design services that can be delivered with Smart House technology.

The research period of Smart House will end with the decade. Commercialization will be under way by 1990 with the construction of about 100 demonstration Smart Houses in the United States and Canada. They will incorporate the production model of the Smart House network, along with smart versions of standard appliances.

How will the Smart House system work? Before we explain its operation, we will first explain how houses are wired today.

4

How Homes Are Wired Today

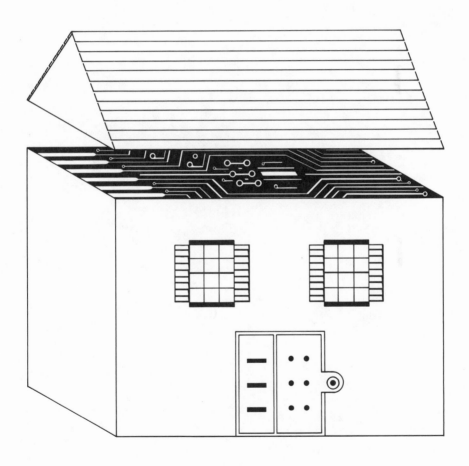

There are now a number of different wiring systems in the home that carry electrical energy. In addition, in homes using gas as an energy source, there is a separate physical piping system to convey the gas to appliances.

The "wire" that connects an individual home with the local electric utility ordinarily consists not of one wire but of three. Two of these wires each carry 120 volts of 60-cycle alternating current (a.c.). The current delivered by these two wires can be combined to deliver the 240 volts that is normally required to power certain major appliances such as dryers, stoves, ovens, water heaters, and large air-conditioning units. Each line also serves individually to deliver the 120-volt service to lights and smaller appliances.

The third wire, called the "neutral" wire, carries no current into the home. It simply performs the function of completing the circuit from the home back to the utility. When a light is switched on in the house, current flows from one of the 120-volt branches to and through the lamp and back to the utility via the neutral wire, creating a complete circuit.

When these wires enter the house, they go first to the load distribution center, as shown in Figure 3. In today's house, the load distribution center is just another name for the central fuse box or circuit breaker panel.

From here, a number of circuits pass around the house, serving outlets in various rooms. Each of these circuits is associated with a fuse or circuit breaker in the load distribution center. Major appliances requiring 240 volts are served by higher-capacity lines running directly to the appliances from higher-capacity fuses or circuit breakers in the load distribution center.

For illustrative purposes, Figure 3 shows a load distribution center with three 15-ampere circuit breakers. From each circuit breaker, current is distributed to a number of outlets, switches, appliances, and fixtures by means of branch circuits. These branch circuits are so arranged that, when any item or appliance is turned on, its power requirement is added to the total load on the circuit breaker serving that branch.

Let us first look at the branch that runs from the top circuit breaker. A lamp is plugged into one of the outlets on this branch. Someone turns it on; the bulb flashes and burns out. This familiar experience can be used to illustrate a characteristic of electrical service that is called inrush.

In the few milliseconds after a lamp is turned on, it draws a substantially larger amount of current than will be required for its ongoing operation. This is true for all electrical appliances and devices. The inrush requirement is especially great for lights and motors and smaller for appliances such as TVs and VCRs. This inrush of current is hard on appliances and devices, which explains why light bulb burnouts often or usually occur when the light is switched on.

The inrush problem has broader implications. It complicates the problem of restoring full power after an outage. When a power outage occurs, most people do not go around turning off lights

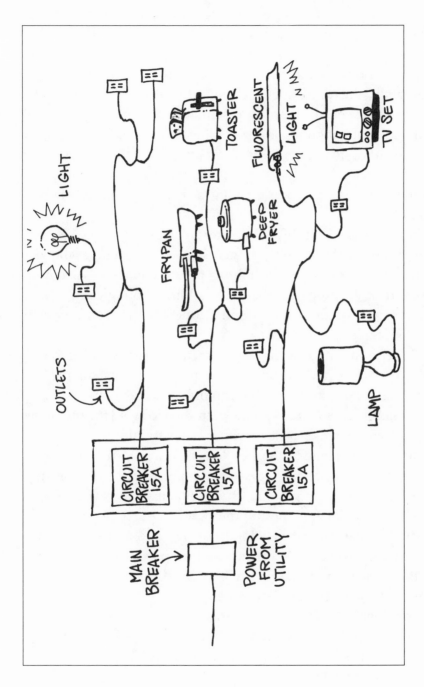

Figure 3. Today's home wiring system

and appliances that were on when the power went out. In addition, the longer the power is off, the greater the number of appliances such as freezers, heaters, and water heaters that will need power simultaneously when power is restored.

Actually, the utility might be able to furnish, relatively quickly, sufficient power for the most essential operations of the home, with full restoration of power coming in increments. But most utilities have no means of implementing such an option. They must be geared up for a full load, including a tremendous simultaneous inrush requirement, before they can restore any power.

Phased restoration of power after outages could be achieved if a communications link existed between the home and the utility. By means of such a link, power could be selectively restored in keeping with the utility's limited but growing capability, powering the most essential functions first, and moving step by step to full capacity.

The continually growing requirements for electrical energy in a largely urbanized America have placed strains on present generating capacity that have important social consequences. Power companies and the public both wish to avoid the problems and issues that are associated with the construction of new power plants. In this context, the problem of heavy inrush load after power outages is assuming a meaningful role in the question of whether construction of new power plants can be avoided.

Now let us look at the middle branch, which serves outlets in the kitchen. Dinner is being prepared, and a deep fryer and an electric frypan are in operation. Two pieces of toast are put in the toaster; the toaster lever is pushed down; and, not surprisingly, the circuit breaker pops.

This highlights basic characteristics of the wiring system. As has been noted, every light or appliance that is plugged in and operated adds to the total current load being carried by the fuse or circuit breaker at the head of the branch. When the circuit becomes overburdened, the fuse blows or the circuit breaker trips. Power is cut off, not just to the offending light or appliance, but indiscriminately to everything on that branch.

Now let us move down to the third branch, whose coverage includes a recreation area in the basement. In one corner is dad's workbench, where he pursues his evening hobby of woodworking. There is a fluorescent light at this workbench, whose diffused light is excellent for illuminating this type of work area. However, the 60-cycle home current causes a "flicker" in this light, which sometimes bothers dad's eyes as he works. Powering the light with current at an increased cycle rate—say 400 hertz (cycles per second)—would solve the problem. So would the use of direct current (d.c.) rather than alternating current (a.c.) to power the light. But dad has no choice. He has to use the one kind of power that is available in the home.

In another corner is a TV set. It is a good one, but, in common with the set in the living room, it suffers from rather odd reception problems. Sometimes a horizontal bar rolls slowly through the picture. Sometimes—for example, when the air-conditioner goes on—a ragged static line dances on the screen. There seems to be no way to get rid of these annoyances.

Rolling bars on TV screens are often caused by the operation of electric motors elsewhere in the home. Motors can feed back, through the wiring system and into the TV set, cycle patterns that are slightly out of phase with the cycle pattern of the current that is powering the set. This all-too-common phenomenon is called electromagnetic interference; it is often referred to by the initials EMI.

Static lines are caused by radio frequency disturbances that result from the armature rotation in electric motors. This is called radio frequency interference, or RFI. These disturbances are transmitted through the air as low-powered radio signals, are picked up by the home wiring system which operates as an antenna for receiving these transmissions, and are dumped into the TV set. As every sports fan knows, rolling bars and static lines seem to lie in wait, attacking the TV picture during the crucial play in an exciting football game.

On the other side of the room, some children are playing with their shoes off. Although they have been told not to do so, the kids have been playing with squirt guns in this room; portions of their skin, clothes, and feet are damp.

In the corner is a lamp whose cord has been scraped against the leg of a sofa, exposing a small bit of the wire. The lamp is not turned on. However, even if a lamp is not turned on, its cord forms part of the live electrical branch running from the circuit breaker right up to the lamp switch.

One of the youngsters steps on the exposed bit of wire in the lamp cord, grounds the circuit, and is shocked and burned. The occurrence did nothing to overload the circuit breaker, which had done its assigned duty of providing power before, during, and after the accident.

Statistically speaking, home electrical accidents are not a leading cause of injury or death in the United States. Unfortunately, it is equally true that as long as today's wiring system is used, it will take its relatively small but inexorable toll each and every year, despite the best that safety engineers and Code officials can do. An unusual set of circumstances such as those imagined in the preceding paragraphs, is sometimes at fault. Murphy's Law assures that unusual things always happen to someone, somewhere.

(The author can remember an instance from personal experience. When he and his brother were very small children, they got it into their heads to cut the cord of a turned-off lamp with a pair of scissors. The author's brother wielded the scissors, and was severely shocked. That he was not badly burned or killed is perhaps due to the fact that they had not been playing with their soap bubble pipes just before putting their brilliant little plan into effect.)

The system that we have been describing is the basic energy system in the home. The piping that brings gas to home heating units, water heaters, stoves, and other gas-fired appliances constitutes another energy system. This system is separately installed, with little or no relationship to the electrical or communications networks in the home other than its link to the furnace or thermostat. Most notably, no advantage is taken of one of the more simple capabilities of modern communications systems, which is to monitor usage and provide safety checks on malfunctions.

In addition to a connection to the local utility for electrical energy, a link to the telephone network is nearly universal in today's homes, and half of all homes are also hooked up for cable TV. Each of these services involves a wiring system that is separate from the home electrical wiring system, and may be installed by parties other than those who install the electrical wiring.

Finally, another system has been entering a growing number of homes to provide security alarm service. This service must be installed by yet another contractor, at yet another increment in cost. The service would be cheaper and more people would probably have it if separate installation and wiring were not required.

With regard to the three major systems—electrical service, telephone, and cable TV—the location of their outlets often bears a decreasing relation to convenience after the home has been lived in and many things have been changed around. A fantasy has probably occurred to many a frustrated home occupant who has found an electrical outlet right where he wants to put a telephone—wouldn't it be wonderful if you could plug anything into any outlet! This fantasy of course occurred to David Mac-Fadyen and to many others who understand that no technological barriers stand in the way of its implementation.

5

How the Smart
House Works

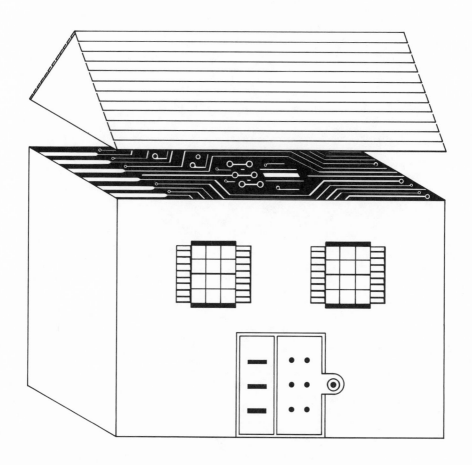

Various details of Smart House technology will be worked out in the laboratory and demonstration home programs, and the system itself will evolve with actual experience and usage. However, its basic features are known and can be described.

Five Basic Features

First, the now-separate electrical and communications systems in the home, including electrical service, telephone, cable TV, security systems, and minor additional wiring such as that for doorbells, thermostats and audio, will be united in a single system.

All outlets in the home will be served by this unified system. The fantasy of today's frustrated home occupant will be fully realized; he will be able to plug any appliance or device, such as a lamp, telephone, or even security sensor, into any outlet.

Second, for homes with gas service, Smart House wiring will accompany flexible gas piping to gas convenience outlets in any room or location desired.

Portable gas appliances can be attached to these outlets. Both appliance operation and gas distribution will be electronically monitored by the system.

Third, delivery of electric power to fixtures and appliances will be controlled and constantly monitored by a low-powered signaling link running between a chip in the fixture or appliance and a chip in the Smart House network interface. The chips and the link between them constitute the key elements of what is called the closed loop system.

In initial versions of this system, small wires will be used for the interconnections of the closed loop. In the future, fiber optics may be used. Fiber is an excellent medium for digital signaling and can accommodate very high speeds of data transmission if evolving applications of Smart House technology should ever require such speeds.

Fiber transmits electrical information by means of a light beam that is not affected by the magnetic fields that can surround ordinary electrical wires or that can be generated by appliances and devices. All possibility of interference with the closed loop signals is thereby eliminated, and precautions such as shielding that will be taken in early versions of the system to insulate the closed loop from magnetic interference can be dropped.

Fourth, the system will include an internal communications network that will link all appliances with each other, with internal control devices, and with the outside world.

As with the closed loop system, fiber may be utilized for this network in the future.

Fifth, the system will have the future capability of delivering more than one type of electrical energy. This capability is called programmed power.

Earliest versions of the system will deliver two types of power, 120/240 volts a.c., and 12 volts d.c.; the latter serves as the system's Uninterruptible Power Supply which will be described below.

It is possible or even likely that, in the future, the system will deliver at least one additional type of power. Early discussions have centered on 48 volts d.c. as a third service offering. Decisions on these future system developments await further research and experimentation in laboratory settings, and further information on consumer wishes and preferences. The author thinks it likely that 48 volts d.c. will ultimately be added to the electrical services available in the Smart House.*

Figure 4 is a cutaway house drawing showing the location of various Smart House features. The drawing will help the reader to envision the actual placement in the house of parts of the system that appear in the ensuing diagrams.

Network Interfaces

The reader's attention is particularly invited to a device in the basement and its associated caption which reads in part, "NETWORK INTERFACES: Located here and in each room." These components contain the all-important chips and are the heart of the Smart House. They must occupy center stage in our description of what a Smart House is and how it functions.

The first step the reader should take is to expunge from his mind the image of branch-pattern wiring that he may still be carrying from having viewed Figure 3 in the preceding chapter. The branch pattern is a correct representation of today's home wiring, but an incorrect one of the Smart House. There is not even a central computer in the Smart House connected to all

---

* Delivery of a second major form of electrical power by the system will require development of a miniaturized switching power supply that will fit into the space designated for power blocks in the network interface. This switching power supply could take the 120-volt a.c. current delivered by the load distribution center and convert it to 48 volts d.c. when a device indicates that it wishes to have this latter form of power. Such a piece of equipment does not presently exist, and the R&D necessary to create it is likely to be undertaken only upon demonstration of significant consumer demand.

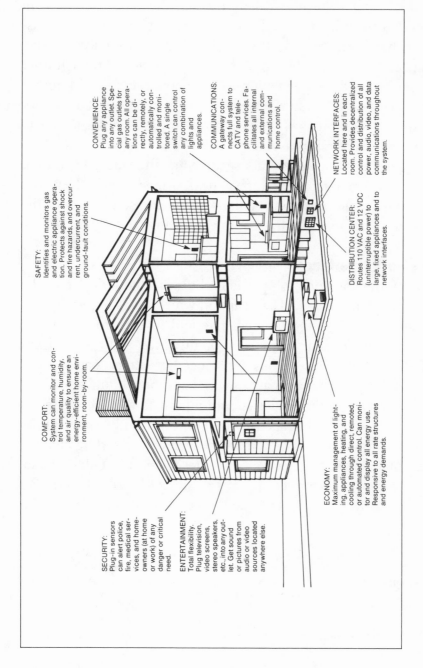

COMFORT:
System can monitor and control temperature, humidity, and air quality to ensure an energy-efficient home environment, room-by-room.

SAFETY:
Identifies and monitors gas and electric appliance operation. Protects against shock and fire hazards, and overcurrent, undercurrent, and ground-fault conditions.

CONVENIENCE:
Plug any appliance into any outlet. Special gas outlets for any room. All operations can be directly, remotely, or automatically controlled and monitored. A single switch can control any combination of lights and appliances.

COMMUNICATIONS:
A gateway connects full system to CATV and telephone services. Facilitates all internal and external communications and home control.

NETWORK INTERFACES:
Located here and in each room. Provides decentralized control and distribution of all power, audio, video, and data communications throughout the system.

DISTRIBUTION CENTER:
Routes 110 VAC and 12 VDC (uninterruptible power) to large, fixed appliances and to network interfaces.

ECONOMY:
Maximum management of lighting, appliances, heating, and cooling through direct, remoted, or automated control. Can monitor and display all energy use. Responsive to all rate structures and energy demands.

ENTERTAINMENT:
Total flexibility. Plug television, video screens, stereo speakers, etc., into any outlet. Get sound or pictures from audio or video sources located anywhere else.

SECURITY:
Plug-in sensors can alert police, fire, medical services, and homeowners (at home or work) of any danger or critical need.

Figure 4. Smart House features

the network interfaces to function as an electronic chairman of the board.

The correct way to envision the Smart House is to see a democracy of very capable little devices, each receiving the same kinds of external input, each able to perform the same functions, and all linked together. The Smart House system is an interlinked chain of network interfaces. Figure 5 is a schematic drawing of a network interface and its connections.

At the back of the interface is a "backplane," which receives electrical power from the load distribution center. Wires from the load distribution center carry current to the backplane of each network interface around the house. The front portion of the interface consists of a number of modules, each of which contains semiconductors.

The left-hand module is called the communications module. This module is linked to the telephone and cable TV systems. As with electrical service, telephone and cable TV service is routed to each network interface.

Next to the communications module is the appliance module. This module is dedicated to internal communications among appliances and network interfaces. The appliance modules in all the network interfaces are linked together with a unified cable resembling the Smart House cable that will be described below. (In addition to wires for the internal communications system, this cable will incorporate coaxial cable for TV and wires for transmitting audio, but will not need the wiring for electrical power included in the full Smart House cable that reaches convenience outlets.) As will soon be described, lights, switches, appliances, sensors, and regional controllers all feed information into this communicating network.

Now we will proceed to the group of modules to the right of the communications and appliance modules. These are called

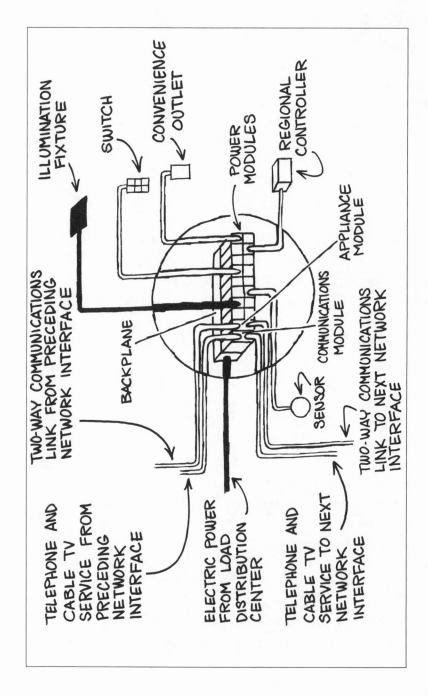

Figure 5. A network interface and its connections

power modules. Each power module contains a chip, and each serves only one outlet, appliance, or fixture.

Viewing these modules, we can see the difference between the branch pattern of today's home wiring and the wiring pattern of the Smart House. As noted above and as shown in Figure 6, each power module is connected directly to some item in the room or area. The network interface can therefore deal with each one individually. If something malfunctions, a power module in the interface can turn it off without affecting the operation of anything else. The configuration of the Smart House network is called a "star pattern."

The Regional Controller

One module is connected to a component called a "Regional Controller." This component is used by the home occupant to tell the system what he wants it to do.

This controller can take a number of forms. For instance, Figures 7 through 11 show various displays on a touch screen. Such a screen could be permanently installed at one or more designated locations in the home. Another type could be portable; it could be plugged into any Smart House outlet and would be recognized by the system for what it is. A portable controller is labeled as item No. 10 in the cutaway house illustrated in Figure 2, Chapter 1. A controller could also be cordless, like the remote controller for a TV set.

Controllers need not necessarily involve a TV display. Other types could make use of push buttons or telephone keypads. Yet others could operate through voice recognition systems or could respond to input from sensors and detectors. Some of these options will be discussed in ensuing chapters. Consumer needs and preferences will ultimately govern the types of controllers that will be available for use with the Smart House.

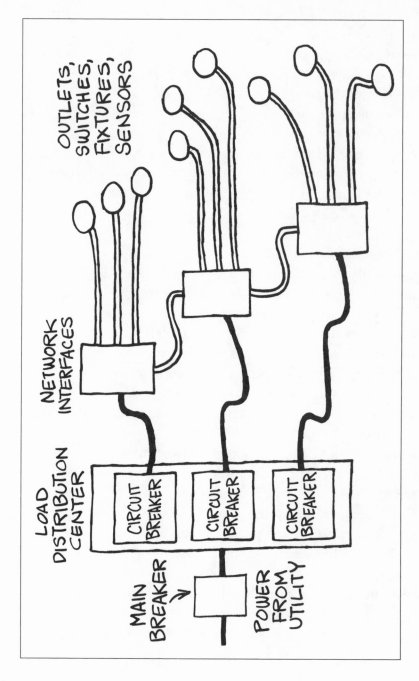

Figure 6. "Star" configuration of the Smart House system

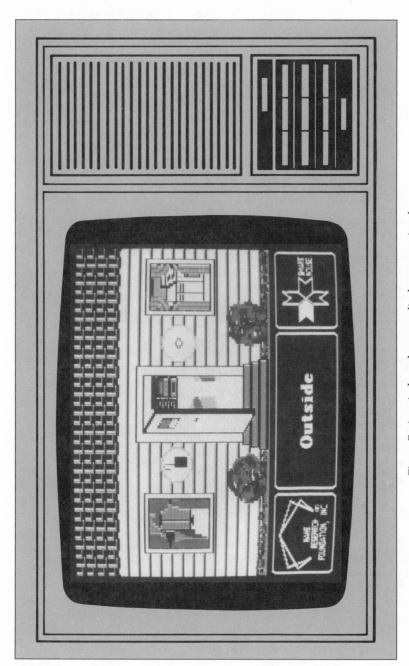

Figure 7. A typical touch-screen display on a regional controller; shown here, an outside security display

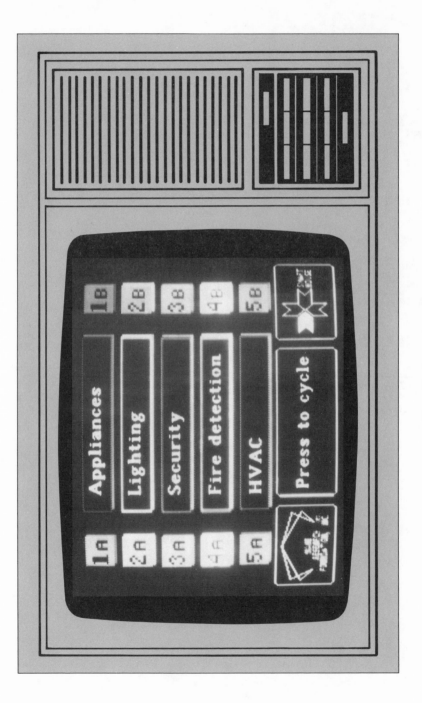

Figure 8. A sample menu

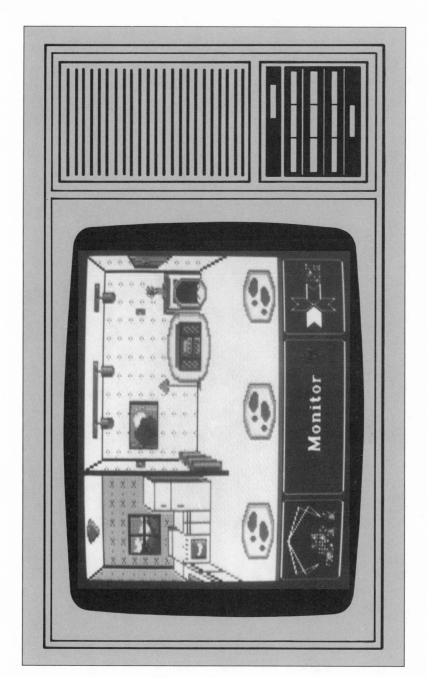

Figure 9. The kitchen and family room in "monitor" mode

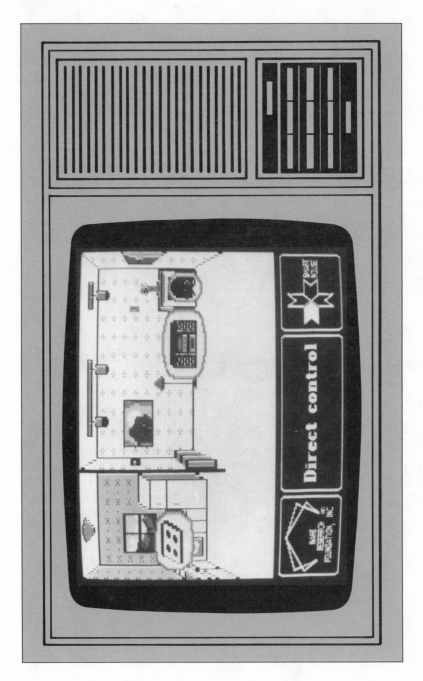

Figure 10. A display illustrating direct control of the stove and stereo

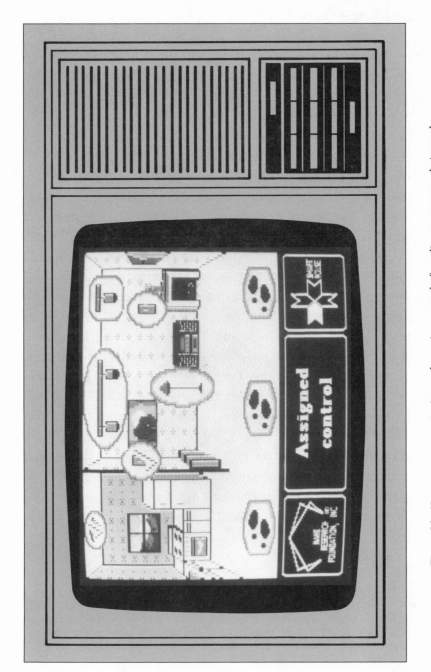

Figure 11. Homeowners may assign and reassign control of appliances to meet their needs

Convenience Outlets

Another power module in the drawing serves a convenience outlet. There would, of course, be a number of such outlets in each room or area, each served by a separate module. Here we arrive at a major crossroad of the Smart House electronic and communications highway. Through the outlet, the smart system "talks" to smart lights, appliances, and control devices.[†] The system brings its full capabilities to this meeting.

The module and convenience outlet are linked by means of the unified Smart House cable. The exact manufacturing details for this cable have not been fully settled, but in general it will contain electric wires for distribution of electricity, coaxial cables for TV, wire pairs for distribution of telephone and audio, and additional small wires to accommodate the closed loop. All wires will be appropriately shielded. An artist's rendering of the Smart House cable is shown in Figure 12.

The outlet will have more prongs than today's electrical outlet; it will resemble the multi-pin plugs of the type that have become common for many electronic products. Each Smart House light or appliance will have a plug that will fit this outlet. An artist's rendering of a Smart House outlet and plug appears in Figure 13.

Except for this plug, smart lamps and appliances will not look different from those in use today. They will, however, differ in one particular—they will contain a chip. Communications from this chip will be understood by the chips in the Smart House network. This is another way of saying that the chip in the item that is plugged in and the chip in the module at the network

---

[†] Today's "unsmart" lights and appliances can also be plugged into a Smart House system by use of an inexpensive adaptor. Appliances will function as they always have, but will not necessarily participate in the new capabilities of the system. Intelligence built into an adaptor might bring some degree of Smart House capability to older lamps and appliances.

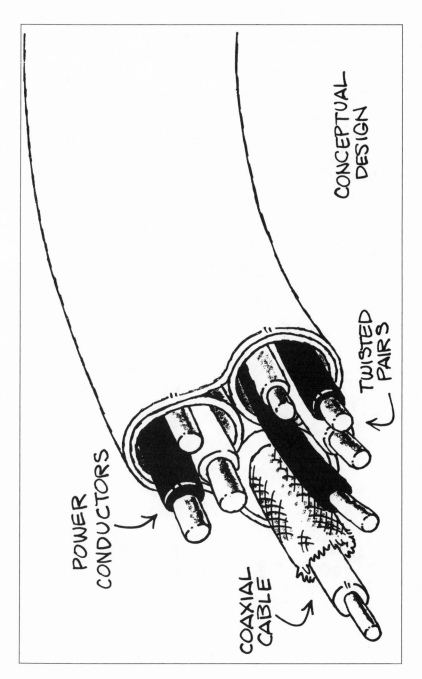

POWER CONDUCTORS

COAXIAL CABLE

CONCEPTUAL DESIGN

TWISTED PAIRS

Figure 12. The Smart House cable

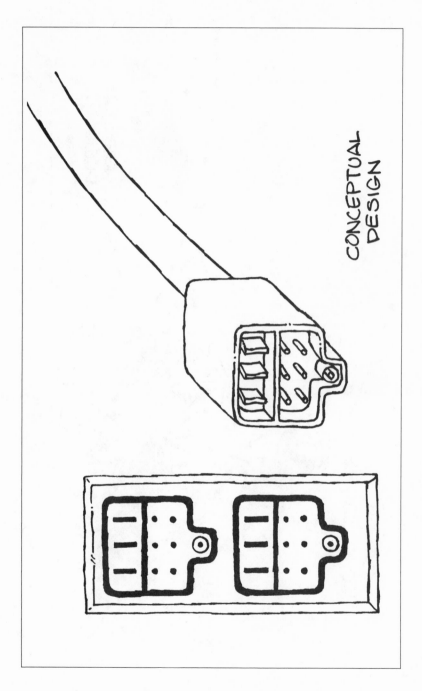

CONCEPTUAL DESIGN

Figure 13. The Smart House outlet and plug

interface have a common electronic language and protocol by which they can share information.

The establishment of this communicating process was one of the central reasons for registration of the project under the National Cooperative Research Act of 1984. The development of numerous systems with numerous languages and protocols would have been a virtually inevitable consequence of a go-it-alone approach among manufacturers, and would have almost certainly resulted in failure of the effort to bring this form of modern electronics into the home.

A smart lamp or appliance can be plugged into the network, but until the item is turned on there is no current in the cable running between the interface and the outlet, in the outlet, or in the cord of the item that is plugged in. If the author and his brother had spent their childhood in a Smart House, their bright idea of cutting a lamp cord with a pair of scissors would have exposed them to no danger.

The Closed Loop in Action

Let us say that we have turned on a Smart House appliance. The chip in the appliance is placed in instant communication with the chip in the power module serving the outlet into which the appliance is plugged. The appliance and the system's signaling circuit are joined in a "closed loop."

The appliance identifies itself to the system as an item that is authorized to receive power—it is not, for example, a child inserting a barbeque skewer, which contains no chip and, therefore, cannot identify itself. It further identifies itself with regard to the circuit to which it should be joined, namely, the main house electrical circuit. It is not a telephone to be connected to the telephone network, or a sensor to be connected to a low-powered circuit.

Figure 14 shows the closed loop in action. Components of the closed loop include the chip in the appliance, a chip in the network interface, and the two-way link running between them. The letters UPS stand for Uninterruptible Power Supply. This is the 12-volt d.c. system, whose primary function is to power the chips in the system. We will discuss this more fully when we describe the load distribution center.

Responding to the information cited above, the chip in the network interface delivers current to the appliance. At the same time it sets up two-way communication between the chip in the appliance and the chip in the network interface, as shown in Figure 15. The two-way communication thus established continues as long as the appliance is on. If the appliance should malfunction, causing excessive current draw, a short circuit, or a ground fault condition, the chip in the interface receives this information from the chip in the appliance. The system responds by instantly cutting off power delivery as shown in Figure 16. The appliance, its cord, the outlet, and the power link between the outlet and the network interface all go dead.

Wall Switches

In Figure 5, another module is connected to a wall switch. In today's wiring, wall switches are wired to a specific outlet, appliance, or fixture, and will turn current on and off only to that item. In the Smart House such switches are wired to a power module. When a switch is turned on, it provides a signal to the power module to which it is connected. That power module then sends a signal to the power module attached to the appliance or appliances that one wishes to control. The question of which appliance or appliances will be controlled is up to the homeowner.

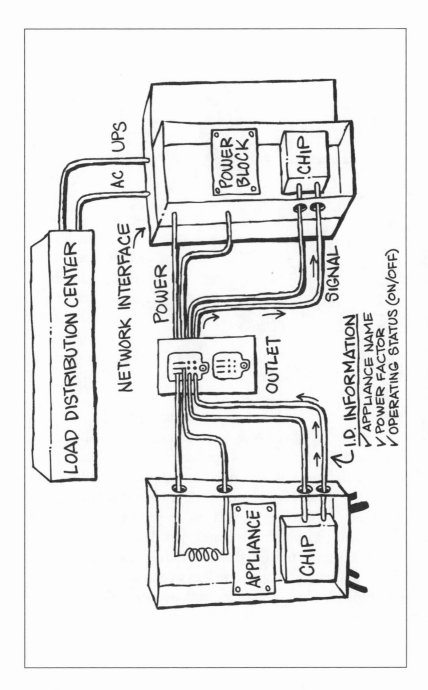

Figure 14. The closed loop in action

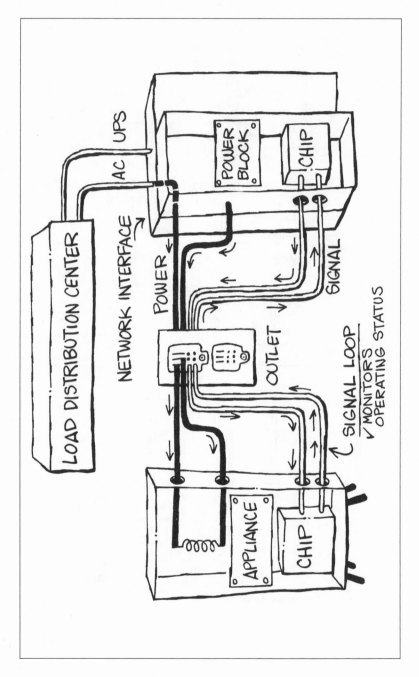

Figure 15.   Communication between an appliance and a network interface

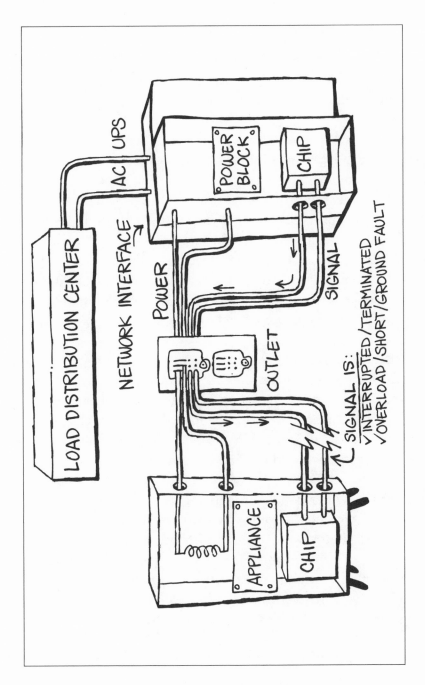

Figure 16. The system instantly cuts off power to a malfunctioning appliance

In all likelihood, wall switches will be assigned at the time of occupancy to suit the occupant's convenience as best he is able to foresee it. When experience and changing home arrangements indicate the desirability of changes, these can be made by the occupant on his touch screen or other type of regional controller.

Telephones, Lighting Fixtures, Sensors

Other items served by the network interface include telephones (which can be plugged into any outlet), permanent lighting fixtures, and sensors for fire and/or security protection. Sensors can be either directly wired to the network interface or can be plugged into outlets. Their status is constantly monitored, and the network can be instructed to respond to changes in the sensor's status in virtually any way that the home occupant may wish. Some options are described in Chapter 8.

The Total System

With the central role of the network interface described, we can now look at the full system. Figure 17 is a schematic diagram of a Smart House network, with the load distribution center and four network interfaces. In an ordinary house the number of network interfaces would of course be greater.

Standard electrical service enters the home at the point marked "AC service." After going through a main circuit breaker, the standard service of 120 volts and 240 volts is passed through Block #1 in the drawing to circuit breakers for delivery to the backplanes of network interfaces. These interfaces can deliver up to 15 amperes to each of the items they service.

Block #2 will deliver the 12 volts of direct current that will power the chips. This is designated as the Uninterruptible Power Supply (UPS) because it will be maintained and continued by storage batteries if and when there is an outage in the main

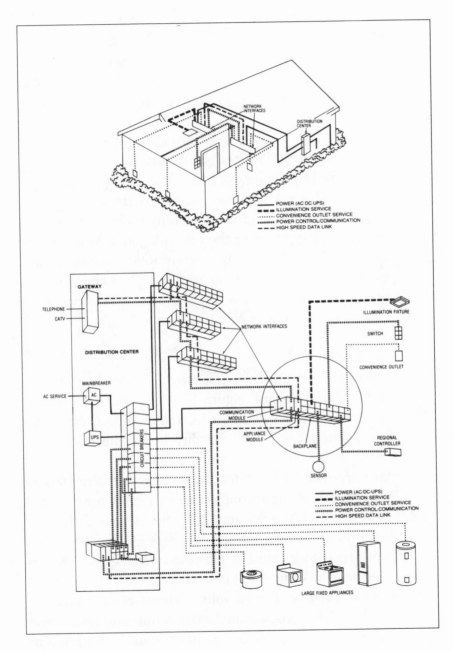

Figure 17. A Smart House network

power. In such an event the UPS will continue to power the microprocessor chips for up to 72 hours and thereby maintain their memories. In addition, it will maintain such low-powered functions as timing operations, provision of a spark for gas appliance ignition, and maintenance of the functions of sensors and detectors.

Through processing equipment not shown in this diagram, electromagnetic interference (EMI) and radio frequency interference (RFI), described in Chapter 4, will be controlled. Rolling bars and static lines should no longer dance on the TV screen during touchdown plays.

As shown at the bottom of the drawing, large fixed appliances will receive power directly from the circuit breakers by dedicated lines. However, these appliances will be controlled by the dedicated network interface shown at the lower left corner of the drawing. This interface can respond to signals from the appliance itself or from other interfaces throughout the house.

In the future, it may be that not all Smart House appliances will employ 120 or 240 volts of a.c. as they will at the outset. For many or most home applications, d.c. is a better choice. Thomas Edison is on record as saying that, in his opinion, no one would do anything so foolish as to serve homes with alternating current. His comment is often cited as an example of the myopia of even the greatest scientists. But in fact Edison was, as usual, technologically right.

Alternating current is superior to direct current for long-haul transmission because it can be managed for power loss, but direct current is frequently better for home use. When electrical service was first being introduced in the latter years of the 19th century, plans called for local conversion of alternating current arriving from distant generating facilities. However, for reasons that may have been a combination of economy and haste, the conversion was usually not done, and ultimately a.c., the better choice for long-haul transmission, also became the home standard.

Many appliances nevertheless operate on d.c. and others would perform better if they did. TV sets work on d.c.; they require a power supply to convert the incoming a.c. into d.c. before it is passed through the set. The same is true of home computers and most other electronic devices in the home. Even a light bulb would last much longer if its filament did not have to endure the added stress of handling the 60 polarity reversals per second of alternating current.

At such time when the Smart House may offer both a.c. and d.c. to power lights and appliances, a.c. motors could be replaced by brushless d.c. motors. If a major appliance such as a washing machine were redesigned to take full advantage of the d.c. option in homes, it would have a d.c. motor that would be smaller and would require less maintenance.

In addition, the speed of the motor and even its direction of motion would be a function of the amount and polarity of the d.c. current flow that it received. This could be controlled at the network interface, and the costly and sometimes cranky transmission that is now required to put it through its paces could be eliminated. A separate timer would also not be needed; timing of cycles could be handled at the network interface.

Direct current could also have important applications in less familiar areas. For example, in the next chapter we will discuss zoned temperature control in homes. If d.c. were available in the home, the speed of blowers used to circulate both heated and cooled air could be simply and fully controlled, from the "off" position through every gradation to full speed, since their speed would be a direct function of the amount of current supplied to their d.c. motors. In so-called hydronic systems, the speed of pumps that circulate hot water through room heating devices could be also directly controlled. Valves and blowers could thereby be added to the tools available for implementing zoned temperature control; in the absence of d.c., they are not easily accommodated.

With these kinds of considerations, we are beginning to move from a description of the system's technology, to a discussion of what the Smart House can do. In the next chapter we will begin to explore some scenarios and possibilities.

6
Heating, Ventilation, and Air-Conditioning

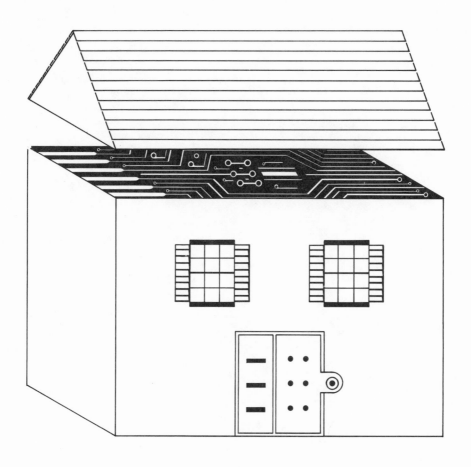

The Smart House has two characteristics that relate to its likely or possible uses. First, it belongs to the group of innovations that could be called watershed technologies. A very substantial demarcation lies between things that could be done before the introduction of such technologies and the things that can be done after their introduction. Second, the Smart House belongs to the category of innovations that have numerous diverse applications, rather than one or a few. Its impact will be broadly based and will affect many things.

Comparison with Cable TV

When considering the future of Smart House, it may be helpful to review the history of cable television, another watershed technology with which we have had a generation of developmental experience. Cable and Smart House both constitute responses to clearly recognized shortcomings of existing systems—with cable, the inability of over-the-air broadcasting to deliver a good selection of channels or good reception to many areas; with Smart House, the problems of simplicity and safety cited in Chapter 2. In both instances, established rather than frontier technology was brought to bear on these shortcomings. With both, the technology employed has capabilities that go far beyond the solution of the immediate problems that it has been called upon to address.

As cable entered the mainstream of home technologies in the 1960s, forecasters drew up scenarios for its future that bore recognizable but only approximate relationship to what we know today. Some features of the forecasters' visions were fully realized; others were never realized at all; and, of particular interest, cable is now routinely used for some things that the forecasters did not envision. The evolution of Smart House is likely to exhibit the same pattern.

Another feature of cable's history is likely to be reflected in that of the Smart House. Cable's uses have evolved, not in a brief time span but over a number of decades. In fact, they are still evolving. Home shopping emerged as a major cable service just two years before the writing of this book. Videotex applications, which flopped when they were tried in the early 1980s, may yet succeed. Cable is a flexible facility that can accommodate many technological developments and changing consumer interests over a long period of time. Smart House has the same characteristics and is likely to experience the same pattern of growth, expansion, and change in its use.

And in fact, this process of growth and change in applications over a period of time characterizes most basic services, including electricity itself. For many decades after the introduction of electricity into the home, its principal use was for illumination; now more electricity is used in the home for running appliances than for lighting.

Zoned Temperature Control in the Home

In certain areas, Smart House makes possible the introduction of improvements in the functioning of houses that have been strongly desired by architects, engineers, and planners but could not be achieved with existing home wiring. One of these areas is the heating, ventilation, and air-conditioning of homes. These functions are collectively referred to in the building industry under the acronym HVAC, pronounced "H-vac."

It has been understood for a long time that present HVAC technology, which uniformly heats, ventilates, or cools the entire home in an on-off fashion, is costly and wasteful. Different rooms and areas of the house have different temperature requirements at various times of the day. A better approach would therefore be to divide the living area into several zones, and to provide heating, ventilation, and/or air-conditioning to each zone in accordance with actual needs at various times.

The layman whose familiarity with these matters is limited to raising and lowering the home thermostat may be surprised to learn that zoned heating and cooling for homes has been a busy frontier of activity for a number of decades. As early as the 1940s, experimental zoned control systems for the home were built and their performance tested. The results were impressive. Energy savings of 20 percent were realized by comparison with night setback of the thermostat in a conventional home heating system; savings of 33 percent were realized by comparison with a conventional system in which the thermostat was not turned back at night.

These and similar findings have already had their impact on HVAC in commercial buildings, where zoned temperature control has become common. But just as intelligent wiring lagged in homes while it was being installed in many office buildings, so zoned HVAC faltered at the threshold of the home. Few problems exist with regard to the creation of appropriate versions of today's HVAC equipment and appliances to implement temperature zoning in the home; in fact, much of the required equipment already exists and is used in commercial applications. The problem has been the lack of a highly capable home control system to secure maximum cost-effectiveness from home zoning. The Smart House system removes this barrier.

A zoned HVAC system will be among the types of equipment that will be built into the first Laboratory Smart House, and research will be done to determine the best approaches to incorporating zoned temperature control as a standard feature of new homes.

An engineering consulting firm retained by the Smart House Development Venture produced the following scenario for heating, ventilation, and air-conditioning in the Smart House of the future.

A Winter Day in the Smart House

"It's 3:00 a.m. and not a creature is stirring except for the Smart House HVAC system. Its heat pump is raising the temperature in the thermal storage tank,* in preparation for commencement of activity by the zone circulators at 6:00 a.m.

"The lower portion of the water tank is also being heated up, for the system knows from experience that this household's demand for hot water starts in earnest at 7:00 a.m. It knows this, for it has monitored the flow from the water tank over the past week; should this pattern change, the system will change its pattern of heating up the tank. It will wait until 6:15 a.m. to turn on the electric resistance heater in the upper portion of the tank.

---

* A thermal storage tank is a large container in which hot water can be stored and circulated through the heating system on demand. Should a utility institute residential time-of-use pricing, the water in such a storage tank could be heated during hours of lowest energy cost.

"At 8:15 a.m. the last occupant leaves without telling the system when to expect someone to return, so the system determines that today is a 'usual' one, and that people will return around 6:00 p.m. Until just before then, it will take no heat from the thermal storage tank.

"At 5:30 p.m. the downstairs zone becomes alive. Each individual fan coil unit starts sucking heat out of the thermal storage tank, via the downstairs zone circulator, at a rate that is proportional to the 'need' of that room. Each room's need for heat takes into account the relative importance of that room, based on recent occupancy history. It depends also on the difference between the actual air temperature and the 'comfortable' air temperature, which in turn depends somewhat on the measured humidity and on the recent temperature history. In this case, the temperature history may imply that the walls are significantly colder than the air, so that warmer air is needed for comfort until the walls catch up.

"At 6:05 p.m. the first occupant returns to find that the downstairs zone is ready for him. The upstairs zone now becomes active, seeking to reach and maintain a temperature that is somewhat below the comfortable temperature. It excepts the guest room, though, for no one has been in it for over a week.

"At 7:30 p.m. the system brings Junior's room up to the comfortable level, for it knows that Junior tends to go there around 8:00 p.m. It will do the same for the master bedroom at 9:30 p.m. for a similar reason. Tonight, however, someone enters the master bedroom at 9:10 p.m. and stays for more than a minute, so the system brings that room up to the comfortable level as quickly as it can.

"At 10:30, the system notices that no one is left downstairs (the lights and TV are off), so it initiates nocturnal setback for the downstairs zone. Each upstairs room will go into nocturnal setback only when all lights are out in that room."

Modifying Today's Equipment

There are four major types of home heating systems.

Hydronic systems heat water and circulate it in a closed loop through room heating devices such as baseboard heating units.

Forced-air systems use a blower to circulate air through a warm air furnace or heat pump. The air is then distributed through the house by means of a duct system.

Radiant systems heat surfaces, such as the panels in gypsum ceilings, to a temperature that is moderately above the ambient temperature of the room or space.

Baseboard electric heaters employ electrical resistance units that become hot when current is passed through them, and which heat the ambient air.

It is possible to install a central air-conditioning system with any of the above heating systems. With forced-air systems, however, it is unnecessary to install separate ductwork. The same ductwork that distributes warm air in winter can distribute cool air in summer. For air-conditioning, the air passes over a cold coil; for heating, it passes over a heater.

Smart House technology can be employed with any of the four types of heating systems, and with air-conditioning systems, to achieve zoned heating and cooling of homes. In general, with hydronic and forced-air heating systems, the function of the Smart House network will be to raise and lower the rate of firing of the heater while also operating valves and dampers to control flow of water or air to individual areas and rooms. With radiant and baseboard electric heating systems, the Smart House can control the setting of each heating unit individually to achieve different temperatures in different areas.

For zone temperature control to be fully effective with hydronic or forced-air systems, a modification will have to be made to today's furnaces, boilers, and pumps. Most of them now in use are what engineers call single-capacity devices. They have only two settings—on and off. When they are on, they operate at one level or speed.

Furnaces and boilers for use in zoned temperature control systems will have a "variable firing rate"—that is, it will be possible to increase or decrease the amount of heat that is applied to warm the circulating air or water, just as one can now adjust the flame on the burner of a gas stove. Variable firing rate furnaces and boilers are actually available now, although demand is small. Improved types at lower cost await only the stimulation of demand by developing the zoning of hydronic and forced-air systems.

The absence of a practical method or system for coordinated control has been the major obstacle to the coming of zoned home systems. Smart House can provide the hitherto-missing capability. With variable-firing furnaces and boilers, and valves and dampers with variable settings all in place, the Smart House can coordinate the operation of all the components of the system, telling each component when and how it should operate to achieve the desired results in each zone through the day and night.

In the Smart House, sensors in each room or zone will transmit information to the network interface associated with the load distribution center and the major appliances (shown in the lower left-hand corner, Figure 17). On the basis of the information received from the sensors, the network interface will instruct furnaces or cooling units regarding the level at which they should operate, and will tell valves and dampers how far open they should be, to achieve various temperatures in various zones of the house at various times during the 24-hour day.

Maximum performance, the engineers state, can be achieved if there are temperature, humidity, and occupancy sensors in every room or zone, and sensors outside the house to provide information on external conditions. The scenario presented above presumes the presence of all these types.

The HVAC system is made complete by adding a simple means of communicating the occupant's wishes and desires. As already stated, various types of user control devices will be developed and tried out in the laboratory and demonstration homes. Securing broad samplings of consumer reaction to both Smart House services and Smart House user controls is a major purpose of the laboratory and demonstration home programs.

The Smart House can make yet another contribution to heating and air-conditioning. Of the various devices cited above, heat pumps and air-conditioning systems share an important characteristic—they both employ compressors. Compressors are major consumers of electricity. Important purposes of conservation and cost reduction could be served by making it possible to regulate the timing of operation of these devices to secure maximum effectiveness at minimum cost.

The System's Flexibility

Intermediate levels of effectiveness can of course be achieved by less sophisticated configurations; for example, one could omit the occupancy sensors. These, however, are likely to be wanted for other applications, such as security, or for functions relating to the needs of older or handicapped persons, that we will discuss in ensuing chapters. In such cases they will be present anyway, and can be electronically linked to the zone temperature system.

This illustrates three characteristics of the Smart House that we will encounter frequently in describing its uses. First, when the basic system is in place, various types or groups of components can be added to it to increase its capabilities, layer on layer. The homeowner can decide what he wishes to spend for what array of capabilities. Second, components or groups of components that are chosen are likely to have a number of different uses and applications, and their cost can be distributed among these applications. Third, because the basic Smart House network will accommodate all kinds of appliances and components, it can support new and future technologies and it can be adapted to changing times, interests, needs, and tastes.

7

Energy Management and Conservation

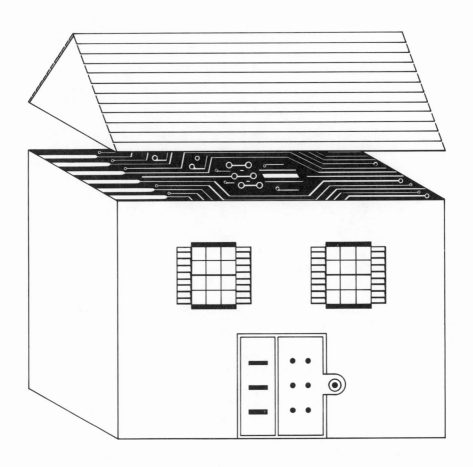

Commercial experience with zoned temperature control and experimental projects in homes both indicate that occupants of Smart Houses will have little difficulty matching the zoned-control energy savings of 20 percent that were achieved as early as the 1940s experiments cited in the previous chapter.

Zoned temperature control, in turn, is part of a larger picture. About one-third of the electrical energy generated in the United States is used in homes. The story of electrical energy use since World War II divides into two periods—the era before the Arab oil embargo of 1973, and the era that began after that date.

The Era of Cheap Electricity

Until the oil embargo, electricity was a plentiful and cheap resource. Utilities conducted substantial advertising and promotion campaigns to stimulate electrical usage. The low cost of electricity featured in magazine ads of the early 1960s pointed out, correctly, that the cost of operating a light bulb in the home had not increased since the Depression.

Accommodating increased usage was easy. When demand exceeded generating capacity, utilities built new plants, whose cost was almost painlessly folded into the rate base because the relatively modest cost of construction was coupled with constantly increasing demand.

The future looked as rosy as the present. According to everyone's vision, nuclear power would increasingly supplant fossil fuel generation as the latter decreased in abundance and increased in cost. Nuclear generation is relatively cheap, and the nation could therefore look forward to having all the low-cost energy it could use, into the indefinite future.

The New Era

As with so many aspects of our economy and society, virtually every aspect of this scene was transmuted after 1973. Power plants that ran on crude oil faced steep rises in the price of that commodity. Coal offered an alternative. However, both oil-burning and coal-burning plants, especially the latter, found themselves in a society increasingly intolerant of the combustion products poured into the atmosphere. It became increasingly necessary to accept the cost of removal of a substantial portion of certain waste products from the gases that went up the chimney. As for building new plants of either type, increasing urbanization, environmental concerns, and adverse community response made it increasingly difficult to find new plant sites anywhere.

At the same time, the great dream of nuclear power collapsed. In the late 1970s, a nuclear accident at the Three Mile Island generating facility near Harrisburg, Pennsylvania, raised public concern to levels that posed immense obstacles to the construction of new plants. Utilities themselves shared the doubts; among other things, no one has to this day found a good way to get rid of nuclear waste. No state, locality, or community wants a nuclear dump, and all have shown willingness to fight to the bitter end in legislatures and in court to prevent one from being established in its domain.

Meanwhile, the cost of electrical power, once so steady and dependable, began to rise. Public utility commissions, who do not enjoy doing things that consumers do not like, often or usually disallowed portions of rate increases requested by utilities. But in the end, the rising cost of generating electricity asserted itself as an incontrovertible fact. Prices went up.

The scene after 1973 was therefore dominated by three factors. The cost of generating electrical power increased; the anticipated shift away from fossil fuels to generate it failed to materialize; and the building of new capacity became more and more difficult. These new circumstances fostered a broadly based concern for conservation. Among other things, utilities invested in research into such matters as energy-efficient home construction, and promoted the use of energy-conserving equipment and appliances such as high-efficiency heat pumps.

The Peaks and Valleys of Usage

The biggest area of interest from the standpoint of plant and equipment, however, is graphically portrayed in Figure 18. This graph, provided by the Potomac Electric Power Company which serves the Washington, D.C., area, shows total load demand on its system during three 24-hour days: January 28, 1986, July 8, 1986, and January 28, 1987. Similar types of graphs reflecting only differences in local climate could be produced for most electrical utility service areas in the United States.

The graph shows an uneven pattern of demand during each of the 24-hour periods. The two January days show very similar contours, with periods of peak demand in the morning and early evening. These two peaks arise from the simultaneous requirements of the subway system during rush hours and the surge

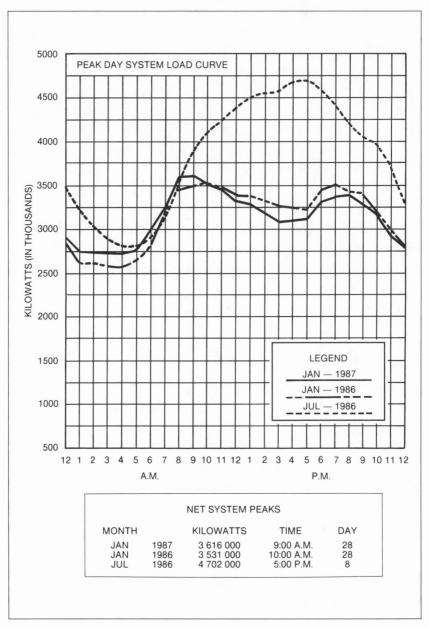

Figure 18. Potomac Electric Power Company graph showing
total load demand for several 24-hour periods

of demand in homes as members of families prepare to leave home in the morning and when they return in the late afternoon and early evening.

Now let us look at the graph line for July 8, 1986. This line looks more like Mount McKinley.

The weather report in the July 9, 1986, issue of the *Washington Post* shows that July 8 was a hot summer day, with a minimum temperature during the 24-hour period of 80 degrees F and a maximum temperature of 97. Only during the early morning hours of 4:00 to 8:00 does the usage curve approximate that of the two winter days. Starting about 8:00 a.m. the curve begins a steep climb that, by 9:00 a.m., has already carried system demand beyond the highest peaks of winter-day usage. From this point it continued to climb during the entire day, reaching a peak at 5:00 p.m. that is about a third again as great as the heaviest winter loads. During the 24-hour period the utility had to provide service in a range that swung from about 2.6 million kilowatts at 4:00 a.m. to about 4.7 million kilowatts at 5:00 p.m.

Almost all the difference between the winter and summer loads is accounted for by one usage—air-conditioning, an amenity that barely existed before 1950 and that has obviously transformed our world in more ways than one. On summer days, commercial air-conditioning loads in the Washington area climb during the morning hours, reach a plateau between 11:30 a.m. and noon, remain there until about 4:30 in the afternoon, and then decline. Residential use continues to move up during the afternoon, peaking at around 7:00 p.m. The dual peak of the two categories of usage occurs between 4:00 and 5:00 p.m.

Utilizing Capacity More Efficiently

Let us consider some questions that are highlighted by the graphs. The lines showing the two winter days reveal that the utility is generally not under pressure during most of the

24-hour period. When demand drops from the twice-a-day peaks, the system has excess capacity that is not put to use.

When electricity was a cheap commodity, leveling off the peaks and valleys of usage was not a compelling issue. If peak loads reached the point of exceeding existing capacity, new plants could be built, with the virtual certainty that the added capacity would soon be fully used. Consumers of course paid indirectly for unused capacity, but the cost was virtually invisible and no one complained.

Now, when electricity is more expensive and new facilities are difficult to construct, the unutilized capacity of existing facilities has moved to the forefront of attention. Finding ways to smooth out the peaks and valleys of usage and create a more level profile has become a top-priority issue.

The problem has been made even more important by the fact that as utilities build progressively toward peak loads, the cost of generation increases. In providing electricity, utilities draw upon their least costly and most efficient facilities first. As the load increases, more costly and less efficient facilities are pressed into use.* In addition, the system is often under strain; brownouts or blackouts may occur, with further associated cost.

In the traditional method of pricing electricity, all these costs are bundled together, and consumers pay flat rates that cover the costs plus a regulated profit. This method has important deficiencies in the context of the new era that is described in this chapter. Flat rates offer little incentive for efforts to smooth out the peaks and valleys of usage. In fact, if anything, they actively penalize the conscientious consumer who would be willing to cooperate by reducing his usage during times of peak

---

* The general order of increasing cost for power plant operation is as follows: nuclear; coal; low-grade crude oil; better grades of crude oil; and natural gas.

load, but who must nevertheless subsidize less responsible behavior by others.

Time-of-Use Pricing

An obvious alternative to flat rates is time-of-use pricing, in which the prices charged for electricity at different times of the day bear a more direct relationship to the costs of generation. Time-of-use pricing can also provide an incentive for consumers to participate in smoothing out the peaks and valleys of usage.

This approach has been used by telephone companies since their earliest years. Few people make telephone calls during periods of highest cost, if it is possible to wait a few hours in order to take advantage of the off-peak rates. In the new era of more costly electrical power, the same approach to pricing is replacing flat rates.

An Experimental Program

Experiments and demonstrations in time-of-use pricing have begun. One of the most extensive experiments was launched in 1984 by Pacific Gas and Electric Company (PG&E), which serves San Francisco and the Bay area. PG&E's program is a relatively simple one; it establishes an "on-peak" rate that is charged between noon and 6 p.m. from Monday through Friday, and an "off-peak" rate that is charged at all other times. The rates, which were approved for the experimental program by the California Public Service Commission, are as follows:

	On-Peak Rate	Off-Peak Rate
Winter	10 cents/kw-hour	6.5 cents/kw-hour
Summer	21.6 cents/kw-hour	5.2 cents/kw-hour

With regard to the summer rates, the off-peak rate is obviously a substantial carrot, and the on-peak rate is a substantial stick, to persuade homeowners to help level off the air-conditioning peak.

In addition to these rates, participants in the experiment must pay an additional $4.50 per month for the new and more costly meters that must be used to deliver time-of-day service. Standard meters, including installation, cost the utility between $30 and $40; meters capable of providing the new service cost between $210 and $220.

The average home in PG&E's service area that uses gas appliances consumes about 250 kilowatt-hours of electricity per month. All-electric homes, and homes that make more substantial use of electricity, typically consume between 450 and 550 kilowatt-hours per month. Heavy users consume more.

By comparison with present flat rates, the break-even point with the experimental rates, including the monthly cost for the meter, is about 350 kilowatt-hours per month. Homes that use more can apply their savings either to reducing the cost of their electric bills or to buying more electricity.

Consumer response has been highly favorable. The experiment has laid to rest any question of whether ratepayers are interested in participating in such programs to help in energy conservation and/or to save money. By 1987 some 25,000 homes had requested and received time-of-use meters. Some civic groups have even asked the public utility commission to require PG&E to install the meters universally, and add their cost to the overall rate base. For its part, PG&E will install 4,500 of the new meters next year, which reflects the maximum up-front cost that has been assigned to the program, but which will not meet the demand.

The PEPCO Program

In the metropolitan area of Washington, D.C., Potomac Electric Power Company launched a special program in 1987 to deal with the problem shown in the PEPCO graph, Figure 18. In this program, residential customers agree to permit the power company to curtail power for a period not to exceed 13 minutes per half hour at peak load times when the utility is under pressure. Curtailment can occur during weekdays only, usually runs for no more than 3 to 4 hours, and is prohibited by the tariff filing to run more than 6 hours. The tariff also specifies that the utility can invoke the curtailment no more than 15 times per year.

In exchange for agreeing to participate in the program, the customer receives a credit of $35 per season on his electric bill. The utility has applied to the Public Service Commission to raise the credit to about $50; the application was pending before the commission as this was being written.

Customer response has been literally overwhelming. PEPCO had expected to sign up 8,000 customers during the program's first year, and an additional 17,000 in each of the immediately succeeding years. When PEPCO launched the program in the late spring of 1987, it had not yet been approved by the District of Columbia Public Service Commission, and customer signups could therefore be solicited only in the utility's service area in the Maryland suburbs. In the first two months, 30,000 people in Maryland signed up.

"I really believe," says Michael Maher, who heads energy management development at PEPCO, "that it isn't so much the money that is causing all these people to sign up. It's that people understand. They agree with the purpose and they want to participate."

The Contribution of Smart House

These approaches represent a good start, but they suffer from two shortcomings. One is the limited capability of the methods and technologies being employed. The other, which is closely related, is the low level of homeowner control, participation, and choice. "What we currently lack," says Brian Brady, manager of energy management technical services for Southern California Edison Company, "is a reliable and economical technology for the utility-customer interface." This key problem will be solved with the coming of Smart House.

First, as already discussed, the Smart House will provide zoned temperature control in the home, which will in itself reduce energy consumption for heating, ventilation, and air-conditioning. The homeowner remains in control of the amount and stringency of the measures that he wishes to take to reduce costs. These decisions can be related to the cost of time-of-use offerings. They can also be temporarily changed at any time to accommodate special situations such as illness in the family, the needs and requirements of older persons, the arrival of visitors, or absence during holidays and vacations.

Second, the operation of certain appliances can be shifted so that these appliances will run automatically at hours when electricity is cheapest. Major appliances likely to be involved include dishwashers, clothes washers, and clothes dryers, which can be loaded at any time of the day; the Smart House can operate them when electric rates are lowest. Water heaters can be operated in the pre-dawn hours to have hot water ready for the morning. For families fortunate enough to have a swimming pool, the requisite skimming and filtering can usually be accomplished by running the filter pump no more than ten hours a day. The time or times for this operation can be chosen to coincide with the periods of low electric rates.

As was noted at the end of the last chapter, the compressors of heat pumps and home air-conditioning units are additional items whose operation could be controlled during on-peak hours. Also, frost-free refrigerators are likely to accumulate frost at increased rates during the summer months. If left to themselves, they are likely to defrost during peak-use hours, but, if controlled by Smart House, their defrosting can be deferred to hours when electricity is cheaper.

In addition, the Smart House can incorporate capabilities that go well beyond anything that can now be done. These capabilities would involve the installation of a two-way communications link between the utility and the home. With such a link, consumers could be given monthly bills resembling those now received from the telephone company, with costs broken down by time of day and possibly by category of service such as lighting, water heating, and air-conditioning.

An approximation of the daily status of the consumer's account during the month could be called up anytime on the home TV screen. Thus, on the 15th of the month, husband and wife could sit down, look at their consumption of electricity for air-conditioning for the first half of the month, and decide whether or not to be a little tougher on themselves during the second half of the month to reduce costs.

Other cost-saving strategies are possible:

- The family could decide to spend no more than $5 a day on air-conditioning. So instructed, the Smart House system could do the rest, deciding the levels of temperatures in various zones, and making special allowance for comfort in such rooms as the dining room at lunch and dinnertime.

- The family could set up a monthly energy budget. The system could report if and when the budget was exceeded, and the family could then decide what steps to take.

- The system could inform the family how well it is controlling energy costs by comparison with last month or with the same or a similar day or month in previous years. For those who might like to be talked to by their house, the system could say, "Congratulations! You made it through a 90-degree day on $5.20!"

The same link could be used to provide utilities with a clearer picture than they now possess of how electricity is used in the American home. Utilities know surprisingly little about the details of how electricity is used; they provide it as it is called for and send a bill at the end of the month. Efforts to learn more involve costly survey techniques that produce, at best, rough or approximate information. "Load research costs us a lot now," says Michael Maher. "With permission from a Smart House owner, we could learn a lot more about how power is used in the home and be able to set rates more appropriately and plan for the future more efficiently."

A communicating link between the utility and the Smart House would make possible two other improvements in utility performance. First, as system loads reached the danger point, the utility could reduce the amount of power available for selected applications in the home. The priority of power reduction could be worked out in advance and appropriate instructions given to the Smart House network. For example, it seems highly undesirable to heat water when no one is in the house to use it and when the utility is struggling.

With this communication and power reduction capability, the utility could move past its power-generating danger point with far less risk of a brownout or blackout. The same method could be used to ease system load for the performance of essential maintenence or at times of unanticipated breakdown, whether or not such breakdown was the result of heavy loads.

Second, if breakdown or failure should occur, service could be partially restored, with the most important applications receiving power first, as the utility progressively recovered its capability.

As we noted in a previous chapter, staged restoration of service would also protect the utility against the substantial problem of "inrush" when power is brought back on the line.

There is an additional technical problem experienced by utilities for which the Smart House provides effective answers. Disturbances can occur on power lines that, in today's environment, can be passed right through into the house. One type of disturbance, called a "spike," can be caused by lightning or by "back EMF (electromotive force)" fed into the power network by heavy electric equipment. Spikes can run as high as several hundred volts. "Surges," which are lower in voltage and of longer duration than spikes, can be caused by problems at the generating source. Either one, but especially spikes, can harm the semiconductors in home computers, TV sets, microwave ovens, VCRs, and other types of home equipment. The Smart House system can insulate the house from power irregularities that occur on the line, thereby protecting equipment in the home and improving the quality of the electrical service.

The Smart House system can also make a helpful contribution in securing maximum value and energy savings from alternate sources of power. Such sources include windmills and solar power generators.

All electrical uses in the ordinary home can usually be accommodated by 160 to 200 amperes of power. Alternate power sources will usually generate less power—generally, from 2 to 30 amperes—and such generation will occur irregularly. The Smart House system can factor this supplemental power into the house's total requirements, reducing the power requirement from the utility in the exact amount that the supplemental power is available. There can also be an automatic trip-over to the alternate power source if power from the utility fails, with the highest-priority needs for continuing power in the home being served first.

An additional possibility that is causing substantial interest in technical circles is cogeneration. It would be well within the bounds of current technology to build a gas appliance that would serve simultaneously as a furnace and hot-water heater, and that could use some of the heat produced in these processes to run a small turbine that would generate electricity. This electricity could be fed into the house power circuit by the Smart House system in the fashion described above. Prototype cogeneration systems and appliances will be tested in the Laboratory Smart House sponsored by the Gas Research Institute.

It should be noted that many appliances and devices currently exist that can perform useful functions resembling one or more functions that can be performed by the Smart House. For example, sophisticated versions of modern clock thermostats can establish a range of comfort in the home on a 24-hour cycle designated by the user, with one cycle being set for weekdays and a different cycle for weekends.

Such devices have significant value, but they differ from Smart House in two respects. First, they are manually and mechanically set. Experience indicates that, after an initial period in which the homeowner adjusts and readjusts them, their more sophisticated capabilities often fall into disuse, and they are operated as regular thermostats. Second, such devices do not interact with other devices and appliances in the home.

"The key," says David MacFadyen, "is integration and interaction of all technologies. Nothing operates by itself, and all interaction is electronic. You give the system simple instructions about the things that you want it to do, and the system takes care of coordinating all the relevant items and appliances to achieve what you want."

This chapter might appropriately close with a look into the more distant future, and particularly at the relationship of Smart House to the evolving technology called superconductivity.

The term superconductivity refers to a change that takes place at low temperatures in some materials, in which they lose all their resistance to the passage of electricity. With superconductivity, electrical currents can be carried without the losses that are encountered today when such currents are carried by copper wire, or when they pass through the increasingly tiny circuits in electronic chips.

The phenomenon of superconductivity was discovered in 1911, but until very recently it appeared to have little commercial value. To achieve it, metals had to be cooled by means of liquid helium to within a few degrees of absolute zero, which is -460 degrees Fahrenheit. However, new materials now being discovered and produced become superconductive at much higher temperatures.

"It is conceivable," says Ross K. Heitzmann, executive director of system development for the Smart House Project, "that eventually, in a time span anywhere from 3 to 30 years from now, superconductivity will be attained at room temperatures, and that 10 to 40 years from now it will be possible to manufacture the required superconductive material at costs similar to those for copper. When that happens, all the rules will be changed for electrical engineers.

"Wire size can be very small, for very large currents. One can imagine a power level of 12 volts to run standard devices and appliances in the home.

"Motors of all types can be lighter, lower in cost, and more efficient. They won't need fans to cool, and they will be capable of very high performance. They will, however, require high starting current, and new designs will be needed.

"Higher efficiency motors could lead to more portable tools and appliances.

"Finally, demand for copper would decline. Pennies may become the only significant copper product."

As this manuscript is being written, advances are being made almost daily in superconductivity technology. There can already be little doubt that superconductivity will be used for certain large-scale applications that involve very high currents in a relatively confined space, such as particle accelerators for atomic research and transformers for electrical power distribution.

Superconductivity might make at least one contribution to the Smart House system itself. It might simplify the designing of the miniaturized switching power supply that is needed to distribute alternate forms of power in the Smart House system. (See Chapter 5, first footnote.)

The level of power that is ultimately decided on for residential applications of superconductivity could be delivered by the system where it is wanted and needed, with 120-volt service being maintained for other functions. It would therefore not be necessary to choose between two technologies, neither of which was best for all usages. Homes with Smart House wiring systems will be able to take selective advantage, not only of superconductivity, but of other technological advances that the future may bring.

8

Living in the Smart House

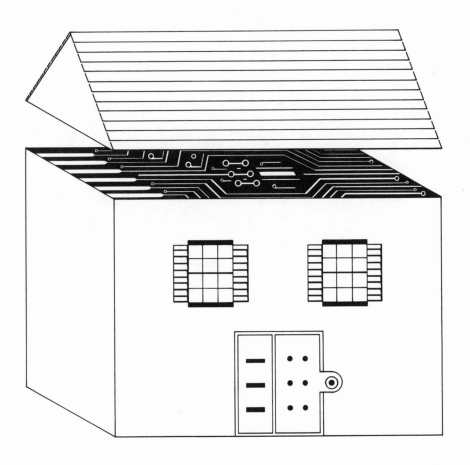

The coming of the Smart House will make it possible to do a number of things better than they can be done today, and will open up possibilities for doing some things that cannot now be done at all. Some of these possibilities will involve the development of new products and services, either through imaginative entrepreneurship or in response to pressures of consumer demand. Some of the foreseen areas of development and usage are described below.

A New Type of Gas Distribution
A consumer technology that can be greatly changed and expanded by the coming of the Smart House is the use of natural gas in the home. In today's homes that utilize natural gas, the piping network reaches one or two locations where the gas appliances are, for all practical purposes, permanently located. Moving these appliances involves reconfiguration of the piping, which is often no small matter after the house has been built. The piping network has little or no relationship to the electric and communications networks other than connection to switches and thermostats.

In the Smart House, the gas distribution system will consist of five subsystems: distribution, control, safety, monitoring, and communications. The network will serve a number of gas outlets located at various points in the home, some of which could even be configured as convenience outlets. Appliances attached to the network or plugged into the outlets will be simultaneously connected to the gas piping and to the Smart House network. A schematic diagram of the Smart House gas distribution system is shown in Figure 19.

Gas distribution will be centrally regulated by a controller/monitor unit. This unit will control the flow of gas on the basis of information received from the appliances and from flow meters, valves, regulators, and sensors. Flow conditions and meter readings will be continuously monitored.

When an appliance is connected to the gas outlet and turned on, it sends a message to the controller/monitor unit via the Smart House network. In this message the appliance identifies itself and indicates its required flow rate. The controller then allows gas to flow to the outlet.

In the Smart House, indoor air quality can be constantly monitored. If it reaches an undesirable level in any zone in the house, fresh outdoor air can be brought in by using ventilation or through an air-to-air heat exchanger, found in some new homes, until an acceptable condition is restored.

The Changing World of Home Appliances

If and when appliances malfunction, the Smart House system can alert the home occupant in the house if he is present, or by phone if he is not. Both gas leaks and water leaks can be detected, and gas or water shuts off whether the home occupant is present or absent.

With the system in place, the home occupant can access it from outside the home—in fact, from anywhere in the world.

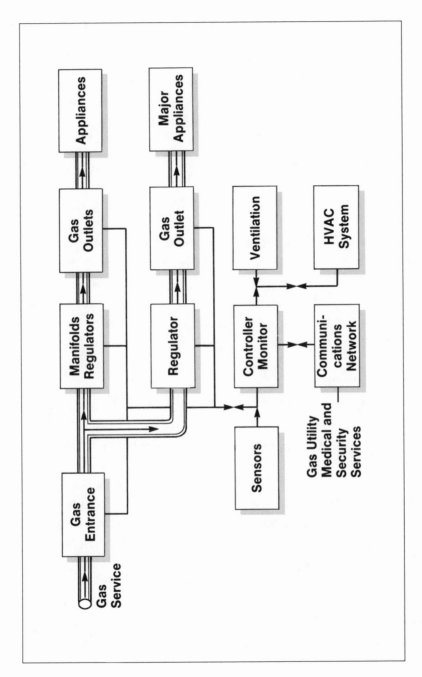

Figure 19. The Smart House gas distribution system

It will no longer be necessary to turn around an hour after one has started a vacation trip to be sure that doors are locked, thermostats properly set, or appliances turned off; inquiries and instructions of this type can be transmitted to the system by touch-tone telephone. From any location, the home occupant can learn if there are any problems at home, and can tell appliances what to do and when.

Potentially dangerous appliances such as stoves or power tools can be locked out of use when no parent is present to supervise children, or when a handicapped person is alone in the house for a period of time (Figure 20).

As was previously noted, a number of basic limitations can be overcome at such time as d.c. power may become available in the home. Appliances designed to operate on d.c. could be smaller, more efficient, and less costly to manufacture. Circuits and devices for conversion of current and mechanical transmissions for changing the speed can both be eliminated.

Security Systems

The cost of a home security system will be reduced since no special wiring will be required. The basic Smart House network will include a security system controller, and sensors in a number of areas of the house.

All systems will include fire and smoke detectors, the former being types of sensors that react to abrupt changes in temperature, and the latter being capable of detecting an increase in the number of ions of certain gases that result from combustion, such as carbon monoxide and carbon dioxide.

Sensors to detect occupancy and motion are currently undergoing a rapid increase in technological sophistication. The sensors are of two basic types. Infrared sensors can detect a change or disturbance in ambient heat patterns. Such changes, for example, are produced by body heat as a person moves around

Figure 20. Smart House childproofs a stove

in a room. Ultrasonic sensors emit high-frequency sound waves, and then "listen" for changes in the returning echo of these sound waves that are caused by movement in the room. Directional setting of these sensors can leave a zone near the floor through which pets can pass without setting off the alarm.

New sensors include types that combine the capabilities of infrared and ultrasonic sensors, or infrared sensors plus sensors that emit electronic microwaves rather than sound waves. Such sensors are controlled by a chip that requires both types of sensors in the device to agree that there has been movement in the room before permitting them to register an alarm.

Highly sophisticated systems employing video cameras are being developed for the home. Such a system, upon detecting an intruder, could make a full video record of his activities complete with time and date. Another technology called image analysis, which is now very costly, is likely to come down in price with advances in chip technology and could be used in home security systems. A system with image analysis will deal once and for all with the question of whether the motion detected in a room involves a household pet or a person who shouldn't be there.

Voice recognition, discussed below, will also be factored into security systems as the technology advances. Arming and disarming systems could be done by voice command, as could the direct activation of alarms by the homeowner.

When the system is armed for protection against intrusion, the security controller in the Smart House network will receive data from the sensors, accept supplementary commands and instructions from the home occupant, perform the necessary logical operations on the basis of the data received, and react in virtually any way that the home occupant may wish.

A central monitoring bureau of the type increasingly being used by security companies can receive the alarm automatically.

At the same time, if the intrusion occurred at night, the system could turn on the lights in the homeowner's bedroom, or in the room that has been entered, or both, and could announce to the intruder that his presence has been detected and that the police are being called. If the home occupants are absent— or even if they are present—the system could also flash all the lights in the house on and off and sound a highly audible alarm in addition to announcing to the intruder that his presence is known. If the homeowner wishes, the same kind of protection could be given to the perimeter of the house; a person coming close enough to look in a window could cause the system to respond.

During the day, when members of the household may be away, the system could activate an audible alarm that could be heard by neighbors, and could also place calls to the homeowner at his office and to designated neighbors in nearby homes.

Additional Uses and Applications
It will be possible to plug a TV screen into any outlet in the house to receive the output of a TV set, VCR, or security camera operating anywhere else in the house. There will be a similar capability for audio speakers to receive signals from any sound source.

A cordless computer keyboard would permit one to sit down in front of any TV screen to do word processing and letter writing. For persons with two- or three-track minds, the screen could have overlay windows in the upper corners, enabling the worker to watch a couple of TV programs without a sound component as he worked. If something looked especially interesting, he could postpone his work, turn on the sound, and watch the picture in full-screen size.

The Smart House could serve as a reminder calendar for all its residents. "Various software packages could keep your schedule for you in various ways," says David MacFadyen. "For example, with voice recognition (discussed below), when you want to enter a future activity or appointment on your calendar, you can do it directly by voice. This could be done at home, or even by telephone from your car. At the beginning of each day, you could review the voice messages and reminders that you have stored for that day. The system could also make voice announcements during the day, such as 'It's time to take your pill,' or 'Your hairdresser's appointment is at 3 o'clock.'

"Another software package would make the same capability available as a visual display on your TV set. Entries could be made with a hand-held controller. At the beginning of each day you could sit down and review your schedule."

Special Needs of Special Groups

Certain capabilities of the Smart House have particular relevance to the needs of older persons and to problems of the handicapped.

One of these capabilities is voice recognition. At this writing, voice synthesis is well developed, and everyone has encountered it in such applications as the time-of-day information on the telephone network. Voice recognition is more difficult to achieve, but nevertheless it is just about to arrive.

While this book was being organized and written, a prototype car featuring voice control of windshield wipers, radio, heater, air conditioner, and windows was shown at a Paris auto show; a doll that recognizes 25 words and responds to about 100 phrases was shown at the New York Toy Fair; a wheelchair controlled by voice commands was being produced by a firm in California; and persistent rumors were circulating that one of the big computer firms was moving along with a word processor that can recognize 15,000 spoken words and put them into print with a minimum of error.

In a Smart House with voice recognition, the system will be capable of recognizing speech sounds and responding in ways for which the system has been programmed. Early voice recognition systems will probably be able to understand only one person's voice. These systems base their recognition on both the pattern of sound and the individual's "voice signature"— that is, the pitch, level, and dynamics of the individual speaker's voice. The speaker will "train" the system by speaking the required words a number of times, and the system will thereafter execute appropriate commands upon hearing these words in this voice.

Voice recognition systems for use in homes can be based on recognition of a small number of words, each of which can serve as an instruction to the system. This level of capability for voice recognition already exists. The network will be able to reply in synthesized speech, and to react in different ways to various specified answers.

Voice synthesis and voice recognition could both be used to serve the needs of special groups—for instance, the blind. Thus, the network could use voice synthesis to tell a blind person when he has left the stove on (Figure 21). It could also use voice recognition to execute various functions for blind persons upon voice command.

The ramifications of this capability are very great for older persons in the home. If an older person should fall and sustain injury or experience some other emergency when no one else is present, the person need only say "Help." The network could provide a programmed reply—for example, "Shall I call John at the office?" or "Shall I call Dr. Brown?" The answer "Yes" would cause the system to place the call, delivering a prearranged or prerecorded message (Figure 22). The system could be similarly programmed for persons with significant medical problems.

Figure 21. System sensors help blind people cope

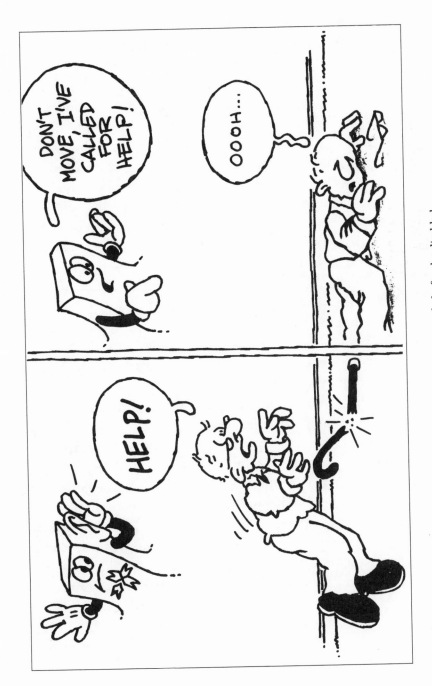

Figure 22. System can summon help for the disabled

Demographic trends make it clear that there will be increasing demand for services of this type. The number of people over 65 is rising steadily, and so is their life expectancy. More and more of this older population is living alone; the current number is 8 million, of whom three-fourths are women. Those who do not live alone must nevertheless often be alone in the house for the regular hours of the school day and working day, when younger household members are either working or in school.

Various types of services are already being established for persons living at home who have serious health problems. These services usually involve small devices which the person can wear around his or her neck, or carry around. In an emergency, the person can push a button on the device, which sends a signal either to a hospital or to a privately run monitoring center via a unit attached to the telephone.

It is of course neither practical nor desirable to place panic button devices around the necks of every older person in America. And with Smart House it will not be necessary. Voice recognition systems can extend this kind of protection far more widely into the general population, combining normal living and freedom of movement with immediate protection in the event of emergency. The capability of the Smart House to receive and understand voice communication, and to respond to problems by communicating with the outside world, may emerge as the technology's most valued contribution to American life.

And of course, whether or not one has medical or other special reasons for having such a system, one could use the same microphone pickups, combined with available speakers, to hold a telephone conversation without moving from one's favorite easy chair.

9
From Idea
to Reality

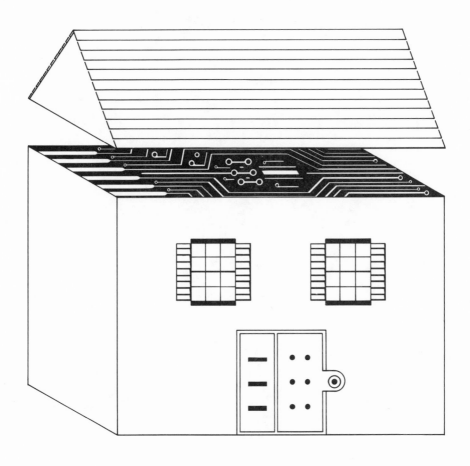

As is described in Chapter 3, Smart House was the first project filed with the Department of Justice under the National Cooperative Research Act of 1984. It was thus a highly novel undertaking, whose success would require a degree of coordination among firms in the building, electric, electronic, and gas industries that was without precedent in the experience of any of the participants. Finding the right organizational path posed at least as many problems as development of the technology itself. A brief description of the Venture and its plans was provided in Chapter 3. Here we will provide some additional information.

Participating Firms and Advisors

Forty manufacturing firms are participating in the Smart House project. They are:

AMP, Inc.	BRIntec Corporation
Apple Computer	Broan Mfg. Co., Inc.
ARCO Solar, Inc.	Burndy Corporation
AT&T Technologies, Inc.	Carrier Corporation
Bell Northern Research	Challenger Electrical
Bose Corporation	Equipment Corporation

Dukane Corporation
DuPont Connector Systems
Emerson Electric Company
General Electric Company
Honeywell Corporation
I-T-E Electric Products
Johnson Controls, Inc.
Kohler Company
Landis & Gyr Metering, Inc.
Lennox Industries, Inc.
National Semiconductor
    Corporation
NOMA, Inc.
North American Philips
Northern Telecom

NuTone Division–Scovill, Inc.
Onan Corporation
Pass & Seymour, Inc.
Robertshaw Controls Co.
Schlage Lock Company
Scott Instruments Corp.
Shell Development Company
Signetics Corporation
Slater Electric
Sola Electric
Southwire Company
Square D Company
Systems Control, Inc.
Whirlpool Corporation
Wiremold Company

As noted in Chapter 3, a number of firms and organizations that are not in the business of manufacturing products for use in the Smart House nevertheless expressed strong interest in the project and sought an avenue of involvement. These firms, which include a number of electric and gas utilities and telephone companies in the United States and Canada, and even an Italian energy firm (AgipPetroli), joined an Advisory Council which meets regularly to receive information on the project progress and to provide input. Members of the Advisory Council are:

AgipPetroli
American Gas Association
Baltimore Gas & Electric Co.
Bell Canada
Bell Communications
    Research
Bell of Pennsylvania
Boston Edison Company

Copper Development
    Association
Dayton Power and Light Co.
Delmarva Power & Light Co.
Duke Power Company
Electric Power Research
    Institute
Gas Research Institute

Hydro Quebec

Oklahoma Gas & Elec. Co.

Ontario Hydro

Potomac Electric Power Co.

Professional Builder
   Magazine

So. California Edison Co.

Southwest Gas Corporation

Southwestern Bell Telephone
   Company

U.S. Department of HUD

Virginia Power

Washington Gas Light Co.

Wisconsin Electric Power Co.

Of these firms and organizations, the Electric Power Research Institute and the Gas Research Institute, acting for their respective industries, have made substantial commitments to the funding of Smart House. In addition to being members of the Advisory Council, they have been designated as sponsors of the Smart House project.

The Role of the Venture

All participants agreed that certain overall responsibilities should be assigned to the Smart House Development Venture. They included general scheduling and coordination of the development work and assurance of technical quality.

An additional matter of central importance that was assigned to the Venture was the development of the common electronic language that would enable the Smart House network and all Smart House appliances to communicate with each other and operate as a unified system. The ability to recognize and use this language would be built into the "chips" in the Smart House network and all equipment and appliances that will attach to it. The Venture will develop and will hold the license for these chips.

As each manufacturer completes his development work, he will pass the license for the manufacture of his particular product to the Smart House Development Venture. The Venture will hold all of the licenses until such time as enough products are ready to enable simultaneous release of the system and associated products. It will then license the products back to the firms that have developed them, telling all of them to begin production.

The Construction Program

The first laboratory Smart House, for which ground was broken in April 1987, is jointly sponsored by the Gas Research Institute and the NAHB National Research Center. In addition to serving as a test bed for technology matters of interest to GRI, the house will be used for component testing and system integration testing of initial versions of the Smart House wiring network, and for testing of initial versions of Smart House software and appliances. Study of human factors associated with the Smart House and its uses will also begin, to determine preferences in such matters as the best type or types of Smart House controllers.

Construction of the second group of Smart Houses, called prototype houses, is scheduled to begin in mid-1988. Several are planned in various locales throughout the United States. They will be co-funded by Advisory Council members, local home builders associations, local builders, and participating Smart House manufacturers.

The prototype houses will contain all the amenities of lived-in homes. They will be used to test advanced system integration and to develop operating features of the Smart House, including the capability for two-way communications with gas and electric utilities. They will also be used in designing and developing installer training programs and for conducting market research.

Most or all electric utilities, gas utilities, and telephone companies that are members of the Smart House Advisory Council have become involved because they believe the Smart House bears an important relationship to the improvement or expansion of services that they offer, and/or to the development of new types of service. In the prototype houses they will conduct technological research relating to new or expanded service offerings and will also secure consumer reactions to new services and ideas.

Research in the prototype houses will continue through much of 1989. By then, the schedule calls for participating manufacturers to be ready with standard production models of supplies, materials, devices, and appliances. As the new decade approaches, the Smart House will move toward the marketplace.

About 100 demonstration houses will then be built by interested builders and developers, which will launch the Smart House on the national level. From that time on, persons living in the vicinity of builders and developers who are building the new type of house can ask for it and get it.

Cost of the Smart House

The exact cost of adding the Smart House network to a new home is not yet certain because products have not yet been developed and their prices are not known. However, initial costs are likely to be offset by operational advantages such as lower utility bills and lower rates for home hazard insurance. The value of the home will be permanently increased and the presence of the network will facilitate resale.

It costs some $5,000 to install the wiring system now used in homes. In the initial stages of production and installation of Smart House equipment, several thousand dollars will likely be added to this cost. As production runs of equipment and contractor experience in installation both increase, the differential between the costs of installing the existing type of wiring and the cost of installing a Smart House network will probably move toward insignificance.

The Coming Decade

The system is expected to gain rapid market acceptance, and, within ten years, to substantially supplant today's type of wiring

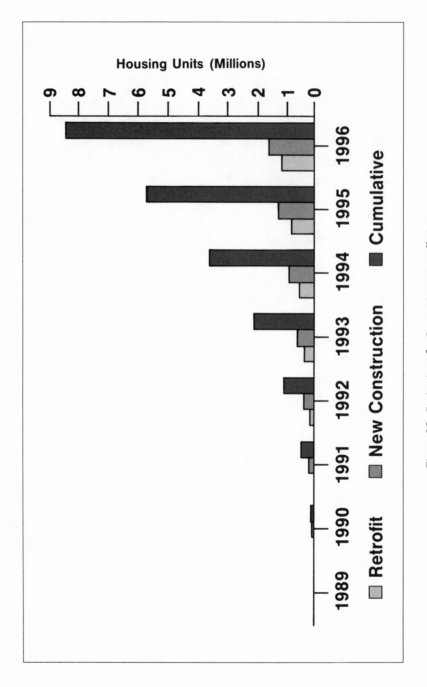

Figure 23. Projections for Smart House installations

in new home construction. At the same time, retrofit versions of Smart House hardware will be developed. It is not expected that the Smart House retrofit package will be installed in a major portion of the existing housing supply. Total rewiring of an existing home will always be a costly undertaking. However, at such time as a new room or wing is added or substantial renovation is undertaken, a certain number of homeowners will elect to modernize their wiring too.

The bar chart in Figure 23 shows projections for Smart House installations in both new and existing homes. As the 1990s draw to a close, a cumulative total of more than 8 million homes and light-frame buildings in the United States and Canada are projected to have the new wiring.

By then, the information age, long stalled at the front door of the home, will have moved comfortably inside. Thomas Edison would be pleased.